Additional Praise for *Flex*

"A must-read for anyone interested in navigating the complexities of leading today. Jeff invites you into his world as a seasoned executive coach, sharing his and his clients' journeys as they learn to *flex* their leadership to thrive personally and professionally. This is the go-to guide for anyone wanting to dig in and lead smart."

—Tracy Duberman, PhD, president of the Leadership
Development Group; author of *From Competition to Collaboration*

"Not just another typical leadership book. Jeff's thought-provoking storytelling has the ability to entertain us while providing profound insights into the complexity of today's leadership landscape. I was immersed from beginning to end."

—Scott Crum, chief human resources officer, MSCI

"What's the next-best thing if you don't have an executive coach to guide your development? Dive into *Flex* by gifted executive coach Jeff Hull. The book delivers an engaging collection of coaching stories wrapped in succinct, profound principles for leading in the wildly unpredictable world we work in today."

—Margaret Moore, cofounder, Institute of Coaching;
founder & CEO, Wellcoaches Corporation

"*Flex* is a jewel! Jeff addresses contemporary challenges leaders face and lays out a clear path forward as workplace dynamics get more and more complex. His vision: a more authentic, collaborative, and fluid organization. Spot on."

—Marcela Manubens, global vice president,
Integrated Social Sustainability, Unilever

"Jeff is a pioneer in the evolutionary work of developing leaders. *Flex* is a thoughtful road map filled with ideas and practices for leaders and coaches to cultivate the kind of leadership needed to thrive in the years to come."

—Eric Kaufmann, founder and preside⟮ ⟯
bestselling author of *Four Virtues of ⟮*

"Brilliant! A must-read for millennials, CEOs, entrepreneurs—literally any up-and-coming leader who needs to know how to take their leadership to the next level."
> —Carol Kauffman, PhD, ABPP;
> assistant professor, Harvard Medical School;
> founder/executive director of Institute of Coaching

"Superb! Jeff Hull has gifted us with the rare combination of lucid illustrative stories woven with the latest science, so that both sides of our brains can be well nourished. An easily absorbable read for anyone from students to managers to C-suite executives."
> —Nina Simons, cofounder, Bioneers; author of
> *Nature, Culture and the Sacred: A Woman Listens for Leadership*

"If it feels like everything you know about leadership is being challenged, well, it is! In his book, *Flex,* Jeff skillfully addresses this brave new world by articulating a leadership approach that is inclusive at its core. Teeming with practical advice, tools, and stories . . . I predict it will become a classic resource for leaders everywhere."
> —Jennifer Brown, CEO, Jennifer Brown Consulting;
> author, *How to Be an Inclusive Leader: Your Role in
> Building Cultures of Belonging Where Everyone Can Thrive*

"Jeff Hull's *Flex* is as practical as it is wise. Hull draws on his many years of experience as a successful coach in health care and other industries to develop a compelling framework that new and experienced leaders can put to immediate use to improve their practice."
> —Amy Edmondson, professor, Harvard Business School;
> author, *The Fearless Organization*

"Rather than advocating for a one-size-fits-all approach, *Flex* emphasizes introspection and adjustment. For any leader willing to take the journey to enhance their performance, Jeff has provided a compass to find 'true north.'"
> —Jeanine Wiener-Kronish, MD, Chair, Anesthesia, Mass.
> General Hospital; professor, Harvard Medical School

Flex

The Art and Science of Leadership in a Changing World

Jeffrey Hull, PhD

A TarcherPerigee Book

An imprint of Penguin Random House LLC
penguinrandomhouse.com

Originally published in hardcover by TarcherPerigee in 2019
Copyright © 2019, 2021 by Jeffrey Hull

TarcherPerigee with tp colophon is a registered trademark of Penguin Random House LLC.

Most TarcherPerigee books are available at special quantity discounts for bulk purchase for sales promotions, premiums, fund-raising, and educational needs. Special books or book excerpts also can be created to fit specific needs. For details, write: SpecialMarkets@penguinrandomhouse.com.

Library of Congress Cataloging-in-Publication Data

Names: Hull, Jeffrey W., author.
Title: Flex : the art and science of leadership in a changing world / Jeffrey Hull.
Description: New York : TarcherPerigee, 2019. | Includes bibliographical references and index.
Identifiers: LCCN 2018057939| ISBN 9780143133094 (hardback) | ISBN 9780525504870 (ebook)
Subjects: LCSH: Leadership. | Management. | Motivation (Psychology). |
BISAC: BUSINESS & ECONOMICS / Leadership. | BUSINESS & ECONOMICS /
Motivational. | BUSINESS & ECONOMICS / Management.
Classification: LCC HD57.7 .H845 2019 | DDC 658.4/092—dc23
LC record available at https://lccn.loc.gov/2018057939
p.   cm.

ISBN 9780143133100 (paperback)

Printed in the United States of America
10   9   8   7   6   5   4   3   2   1

Book design by Elke Sigal

for my KP

CONTENTS

Contents

Introduction

The weather was nearly perfect. The view of San Francisco from the air must have been stunning—and exciting—for the seventy students who were traveling from Seoul to attend a music exchange program. But in the final moments, everyone on that Boeing 777 sensed something was amiss. As survivors recounted later, the ground outside their windows looked close enough to walk right out onto the seawall below. At exactly 11:28 A.M. on the morning of July 6, 2013, Asiana Airlines flight 214 crashed into the wall that separates San Francisco Bay from the runway. Miraculously, all but three of the passengers survived, but there were hundreds of serious injuries.

In the aftermath of the first deadly crash in the United States in five years—and the first for a 777—the three pilots struggled to get their stories straight.

Even in the best of conditions, the roles of the flight crew can vary greatly depending upon seniority, the choice of seat, and who is designated the pilot in command. Yet there is one thing that they had trained for: When you see something that's not right, you speak up—even if it means contradicting a senior officer, or the pilot manning the controls. The fact that they were fast approaching the wall before they had cleared the runway was evident within the cockpit and even from miles away—the disastrous landing was caught on video by bystanders from across the bay. The pilot at the controls said later that he was "uncomfortable" with making a "visual approach"; as the automatic pilot controls malfunctioned, he had to look out the window, gauge the timing, speed, and elevation, and land the plane the old-fashioned way. But neither of the ancillary pilots spoke up at the time, even though one of them, a seasoned veteran with thousands of hours of flight time on large jets, noticed that they were coming in too fast and low for a good landing. When the third pilot shouted out "Go round," meaning do not land and take the plane around to try again, they were only four seconds from impact. Too little, too late. Why did no one speak up earlier?

Three thousand miles away, on an equally sunny afternoon, in the bowels of one of America's largest and most prestigious hospitals I was interviewing a seasoned anesthesiologist about the very topic that caused flight 214 to crash. Pure coincidence, of course, but memorable nonetheless. May Pian-Smith, a specialist in OB-GYN clinical practice, had just finished publishing the results of one of her first studies on the risks inherent within the hierarchical dynamic in a typical operating room. I had just observed my first operation, during which I sat in awe of the complex dance taking place between the surgeons, the anesthesiologists, the nurses, and the technicians who run the multiple computers and robotic equipment that make up today's operating rooms.

The twentysomething man on the table was awake and chatty as they rolled him in. Tom was proud of the tattoos that all the nurses were ooing and ahhing over. His chatter diminished when one of them brought up the reason he was there: a highway motorcycle accident during which he had been thrown fifty feet, breaking his clavicle, after trying to outrun a tractor trailer. As the anesthesiologist put him under, his last words were "Thanks, Docs. I'll be more careful next time...."

Truth be told, I was more interested in observing the hierarchy, which was clear from the moment I entered the room, than reflecting on the testosterone-fueled road rage that may have caused this situation. The attending surgeon was top dog even though he never lifted a knife. A resident surgeon performed the surgery, barking orders to the OR nurses, the CRNA (certified registered nurse anesthetist), and the attending anesthesiologist. The attending surgeon admonished the resident for sewing up the patient a bit too fast so that the stitches appeared, at least to him, a bit sloppy; the attending was known for meticulously neat stitches, and this resident's work—and any scars that remained—would forever carry his signature.

Later, when I was discussing this dynamic with May, one of the lead anesthesiologists in the training of new docs in the OR, I asked, "What happens when one of the staff disagrees with the attending surgeon? Do they ever speak up?" I was familiar with the truism that your typical surgeon does not appreciate being contradicted—probably not in general, and certainly not during an operation. That's when May shared her research on the challenges of minimizing surgical and physician errors. The facts were sobering. Hundreds of postmortem studies of OR mishaps showed that the sacrosanct power of the lead surgeon all too often led to avoidable, sometimes harrowing, mistakes when other members of the team failed to speak up.

The good news, as May recounted, was that team dynamics in hospitals across the country—and the globe—were evolving. Since

2001, new training programs and protocols had come into play, and simulation programs were put in place to educate young physicians on how to work in teams, with respect for the traditions and the hierarchy, but equal respect for observing, acting, and speaking on behalf of the patient. If something is amiss, and someone lower on the totem pole sees it, they are encouraged—no, *obligated*—to speak up. The days when no one would speak up in the face of the alpha dog are dwindling.

Of course, tradition dies hard. Despite a fresh awareness of the importance of teamwork, it naturally remains a challenge for junior or less experienced clinicians to speak truth to power. As I observed the dance of surgery firsthand, I could totally understand. I know that I would be hard-pressed to speak up in the face of the dominating surgeon. He was clearly in charge, and the rest of us were there to do his bidding. For the most part, that is exactly as it should be. Until it isn't.

For his bestselling book *Outliers,* Malcolm Gladwell researched fatal crashes in which pilot error was the determining factor. He found that the core problem with the cockpit dynamic was that many cultures have such a deeply entrenched respect for hierarchy and the wisdom of experience, that no matter how well they are trained, junior officers would defer to a superior, even if there was something noticeably awry. His assessment was that many of these crashes would not have happened if the pilots were not only trained, but also acculturated to focus on *what* was right and not so much on *who* was right.

Gladwell was making an astute observation about how deeply engrained our cultural values can be; and there will always be, under certain circumstances, a need for decisive leaders who can handle tough situations, make quick decisions, and save the day. But I think reluctance to stand up to a leader is not just a cultural artifact; it's just plain human, a result of thousands of years of patriarchal norms.

Fortunately, as May's research indicates, and my experience at dozens of hospitals, nonprofits, and corporate organizations—from start-ups to the *Fortune* 100—confirms, the world is changing. Alpha types often still run the show—but they are also a dying breed. Organizational models comprised of circles and networks are rapidly replacing the old standby pyramid.

Research on the values of millennials, usually defined as the cohort born between 1981 and 1996, indicates that—like every generation—they can be complex. In general, they desire less hierarchy and more of a meaningful, collegial, partnership-oriented culture and work environment. Yet about 70 percent also say they want guidance from their leaders and appreciate following the vision of a seasoned expert. They want mentoring from someone with expertise. Basically, they want a boss, but not an alpha: a beta boss. By "beta," I don't mean the stereotypical moniker for someone who is passive or subordinate. There is an emerging recognition that people with less directive, less authoritative styles can be equally valuable and impactful in leadership roles. In her bestselling book *Quiet*, Susan Cain shows that even though we live in an extroverted culture, introverts can be surprisingly effective leaders, too. Beta is a shift in mind-set from a goal-oriented, top-down figuration to a growth-oriented, process-based one. When we live in beta, we are in flux, always improving, and always aware of the need to disrupt the status quo.

The alpha leader seeks to rise to the top and is focused on delivering a result. This emphasis on a finished product is not a recipe for innovation in a world where the next great thing may be quickly considered old hat, where the best ideas may spring forth from any corner of an organization. Any true entrepreneur is never satisfied with the results of her output, no matter how successful. The very nature of entrepreneurialism represents a commitment to and a passion for improvement, for harnessing creativity and enhanced productivity. Alphas want to win; betas want to grow. Alphas want to control; betas want to collaborate, share, and engage over and over again.

We will always have alpha dogs, but the rise of the beta leader is about shifting our mind-set toward more effectively navigating a world of relentless change, one in which traditional emblems of success, including reaching the top of a corporate ladder, feel quaint and out of date. Beta means being comfortable in a state of constant growth, not aspiring so much to ascend the hierarchy and dominate from above, but to lead from anywhere, anytime.

When Google introduced Gmail, in one fell swoop they changed the whole meaning of the words "beta release." Typically, software developers held off on the release of a new product to the public until—after many iterations in a controlled and limited format—they reached a point where the product was considered "ready." Beta meant that engineers were still tweaking and fixing bugs, and generally considered the product unfinished. A company would never consider releasing a beta version of a product to the public.

Google changed all that. It started as a quiet revolution (typical, as we'll see of beta leaders) with the release of the beta version to a limited number of users, while encouraging feedback on what worked, what didn't work, what users wanted to see, what they liked, and what they didn't like. Also, Google asked these early adopters to recommend the product to their friends. In 2004, this was all a risky bet, as many reviewers and executives (even within the company) were concerned that the public would detect flaws in the software and reject it. Yet because Google was up-front about the beta nature of Gmail and their request for feedback, they were not only *not* hurt by the fact that their product wasn't complete, their reputation was enhanced on two fronts: 1. They were viewed as honest brokers, and rather than being disappointed, users felt respected; 2. Users felt special in that they were being encouraged to, in effect, join the team at Google to enhance and improve the product.

This was a profound change in the way that innovation came to the public. The company shifted away from a goal of perfection—from reaching the "alpha state"—to a loop of improvement. Google doesn't promote its products as complete or flawless. Gmail is *continuously* in beta. This is a perfect metaphor for the leadership landscape today. Beta leadership is, at its core, about reciprocity. It parallels the cultural shift toward a shared economy. Just as many of us no longer have just one career, or even five, leadership is no longer about climbing a ladder to reach a pinnacle of success.

We Are All Millennials

A few years ago, I submitted a proposal for an article in *Harvard Business Review* about the shifting values and attitudes of millennial leaders. The response I received back was telling: "Great ideas for describing the brave new world of work and leadership, Jeff, but we don't focus so much on 'millennials' these days. We're not finding the demographic distinctions very helpful. Besides, there is already a ton of material out there on how the so-called millennial generation is different from Xers and boomers . . . but we are not so sure." And, truth be told, neither am I. No matter their age, my clients are more similar than different. Sure, the younger folks grew up with smartphones and social media, but most of us have become accustomed to using them. We are all experiencing the news cycle speeding up, the addictive qualities of our screens and the constant availability they demand, the shrinking of global and cultural distances, and the struggle for work-life balance.

Ultimately, we are becoming more alike. We live in an age of convergence, with many distinctions dissolving. Job security is long gone, a vestige of the twentieth century. Studies show that millennials and the emergent Generation Z (those born late 1990s through 2014) are more focused on meaning and purpose than financial gain; they are socially aware, health conscious, and interested in making a difference. But is it possible that these values are just the baby boomers' dreams coming home to roost? Most of my older clients, having put aside their more altruistic values in order to make a living, still harbor a deep-seated passion for finding meaningful and fulfilling work, not just a paycheck. These days, we are all millennials.

When I first started working with professionals in need of coaching—or what I called "counseling" in the midnineties—I was in HR at the information tech and strategy consulting firm Booz Allen. Many of the senior associates and principals would come to me with their fears and desires about how to become a partner, which was the holy grail of the consulting world. Firms such as McKinsey, BCG, Bain, and Booz represented the top echelon of recruiters at MBA schools: Everyone wanted to work for a consultancy. If you were lucky enough to get hired as an associate, the path was clear: Assuming you did great client work, were loved by your boss, mentored your juniors, and worked ninety hours a week on all corners of the globe, you climbed the ladder two years at a clip. Four years later, you would become a principal—a lofty title that meant running projects, less drudge work, and the entry into "selling mode." Finally, the key to making partner was the ability to shift gears from doing projects to running projects to selling projects. Leadership skills didn't actually play a big role, whereas being a great relationship manager was crucial: cultivating a network of clients who clung to your every word and viewed you as their go-to consultant.

Teaching master's-level grad students in marketing and business at New York University today, I see professionals from all walks of life who aspire to success but know that there are fewer and fewer ladders to climb. The path to leadership even at the most traditional companies—GE, GM, Disney, and the like—has been ineluctably altered. In fact, the very definition of success has changed. What is most noticeable is that leadership is no longer the province of a few in the cavernous offices of the C-suite (which still exists but is quickly becoming an anachronism). Leadership happens earlier. Leadership matters more. Leadership is necessary at all levels: from bottom up, top down, and middle out. And our classic understanding of leadership itself— authority, charisma, expertise—is no longer the only game in town.

Today, leadership is expected of—and available to—the many, not just the few, and this creates both opportunity and disruption. The kind of leader that will succeed in today's fast-moving, mercurial workplace is not all alpha or all beta. You need to build leadership muscles for both strength and agility, recognizing when to adapt and shift your approach to match the situation. In a word, great leaders learn to *flex*. I admire my grad students who clamor to run their own companies, be senior execs at start-ups, manage teams, and build business units before they hit thirty. Organizations must be adaptable and nimble, and providing younger professionals opportunities to lead and skip the "drone" phase is a sign of positive evolution. Yet, as anyone who has taken up the gauntlet to lead at any level knows, there will be hiccups along the way. *Flex* is here to help.

Perhaps you can relate to some of the leadership challenges my real-life clients are facing in this tumultuous world:

An accomplished scientist with a PhD in genetics, Mariza was promoted to senior director of R&D at a global pharmaceutical firm, only to discover that while she sat in a quiet suburb of Philadelphia, her direct reports were based in Norway, France, Ireland, India, Sri Lanka, and Australia. Her local team had been dissolved and there was no travel budget for at least a year. Her first question: "How do I lead people I never get to meet?"

Recruited into a two-year-old e-commerce start-up as its first director of product management, Jason found himself reporting to three executives, all of whom were younger than he was. Instead of directly managing anyone, he was expected to "pull in people from other teams as needed." He wanted to know, "How do I lead people who work for me only if they feel like it?"

Thrilled to be chosen as the first director of a newly formed division of critical care at an Ivy League academic hospital, Raquel soon discovered that, even though more than one hundred physicians worked at least part-time in the ICU, none of them considered themselves her reports, as they also belonged to other divisions—cardiac care, general surgery, pain medicine—where the chains of command were already entrenched. Her lament: "How do I lead people who already report to someone else?"

Hired at a fast-growing retailing company as the senior director of performance marketing, Julie was told by HR to submit to "360 feedback" after less than six months in the role. Rumors were rampant that she needed to improve her "likability index." Frustrated, she asked me, "How am I supposed to succeed when I'm constantly under the micro-scope of employee opinion surveys?"

Welcome to the new leadership. But there is good news: All the stories above had happy endings. These unstructured environments present fresh challenges, but with a firm foundation of knowledge and practice in the six domains that matter—Flexibility, Intentionality, Emotional Intelligence, Realness, Collaboration, and Engagement—anyone with the desire to lead and the willingness to try out new approaches can succeed beyond their wildest dreams. I know this to be true, because my model is based, first and foremost, on reliable science, and on something even more useful—direct observation. In the pages that follow, you will meet leaders like Mariza, Jason, Raquel, and Julie, who learned how to effectively navigate today's workplace dynamics.

The Birth of a Model

What I remember about my first encounter with Mark was the smell. Leadership came later. An orthopedic surgeon in his midthirties, Mark and I met when he joined a development program for up-and-coming team leaders in the surgical, anesthesia, and pain medicine division of a major Ivy League health care organization. During the coaching phase of the training, Mark enthusiastically recommended that I shadow him for a couple of days. He was not only open to feedback; he was a rare breed: He wanted it. Unlike the surgeon I observed in 2013, Mark was a beta, through and through.

Our day started at 5:30 A.M. with a quick Starbucks and even quicker lesson in how to suit up and scrub in for surgery. When we walked into the OR, it was already packed with nurses, technicians, an anesthesiologist, a couple of residents, and, of course, the patient.

Mark encouraged me to watch closely, so I could see him and his team in action. I took it all in, this universe of high-tech medicine, and I watched, wide-eyed with anticipation, as the patient was put under.

And then there was this enormous geyser of blood.

Everyone else took it in stride, but as blood flowed seemingly unabated, I felt dizzy and light-headed. Just before I thought I might faint, it got worse: an overpowering stench hit my nostrils. Mark, dripping scalpel in hand, turned to me and whispered, "Just breathe, Jeff, take some deep breaths, and sit. You will be okay." A nurse handed me a cup of cold water. Slowly, I felt my own blood circulating back into my arms and legs. And that's when I witnessed what I would call "post-heroic leadership" in action, a sort of orchestral performance, with Mark conducting in a way that brought out the best in each player. It was exciting and unnerving, but also an honor to see these world-class musicians of medicine do what they did best. Much like the surgery I had observed a few years earlier, Mark was clearly the alpha. But the tone was different, with less emphasis upon hierarchy and more of a sense of teamwork, reciprocity, and respect for the talent and expertise of everyone in the room. Mark was the conductor, but each nurse, anesthetist, and technician had a key role to play.

Three hours and two surgeries later, I tagged along as Mark took a quick walk past the maternity ward on his way to a meeting. When I asked him why the detour, he exclaimed, "I always stroll past this window, glance in, and connect for a moment with the miracle of new life. It helps me drop the stress of the OR and slow down, and enter whatever is next with good humor and gratitude."

Mark entered the meeting with literal and figurative scrubs off and tie on. He looked at spreadsheets and discussed budgets, actively listening and sharing with his colleagues. The hierarchy of the OR was gone, replaced with a feeling of camaraderie. Even when there was a disagreement, Mark remained reflective, focused, and attentive to the opinions of others. In the transition from operating theater to boardroom, I witnessed Mark's behavior shift from the alpha mode needed to orchestrate the operation back to his natural beta style as a consensus builder.

And then we were off again, this time to a sandwich date in the courtyard with an attending physician, just out of residency and feeling pressured, overwhelmed, and inadequate. I stayed quiet as Mark counseled, coached, and ultimately cajoled this stressed-out new doc back to work with a smile on her face. What was most noticeable was Mark's ability to empathize with his young colleague and communicate with her in ways that were clearly inspiring. In this context, Mark was not lofty or strategic, but earthbound and emotive. The day continued with more meetings and check-ins on patients and patients' families, as he moved with agility from authority figure to teammate to coach to family therapist, navigating a surfeit of roles with humility and humor. Observing Mark effortlessly navigating from one encounter to the next, it dawned on me that his ability to adjust his style based on context was key to his effectiveness as a leader. Mark embodied both alpha and beta qualities, all in the space of one day. This revelation kick-started the journey that culminated in the FIERCE model that underpins this book. But before Mark, as talented as he was, could become my role model for how to flex, I had work to do.

My first step was to go back and revisit the hundreds of coaching assignments I had done over the years. Having coached physicians like Mark, as well as executives at major banks, software firms, pharmaceutical companies, start-up e-commerce firms, and nonprofits, I had a treasure trove of data from both seasoned and up-and-coming leaders. Numerous themes surfaced again and again—characteristics that many, if not most, of my clients had received feedback on or suggestions to change. They fell into broad categories:

- Bossing, and not enough listening.
- Too much data, and not enough passion and inspiration.
- Being too reserved, and not expressing enough empathy, transparency, and openness.
- Independence and reliance on expertise, and not enough teamwork and collaboration.
- Too much oversight—what we often call "micromanagement"—and not enough empowerment.
- Too much or too little structure—a lack of alignment between structure and purpose.
- Energy for results, but not enough support for creativity and innovation.

Almost all of my coaching assignments touched on decision-making style, communication, emotional intelligence, authenticity, collaboration, and/or engagement.

My next step was to survey my colleagues. I wanted to be sure that my client roster of twenty years was not an outlier. What did other executive coaches focus on? What themes came up with regularity? Then I dove into the research on coaching and leadership effectiveness to see how it had evolved over the past decades. I discovered that science bears out the basic premise that I had observed in my practice: The heroic leader is dead. As one of my clients put it, "The myth of the white knight who rides in on his horse to save the day, well, Jeff, we don't see many of those around here anymore. I think they are slowly being put out to pasture."

The key to success in this post-heroic era is agility: the ability to shift and adjust your style as needed, to influence, motivate, and inspire others, regardless of your title or position, or how big your office may be. Hundreds of studies have found that what is commonly called authentic or transformational leadership—what I call "post-heroic" or "beta"—is based on six core dimensions of leadership agility within three categories of power available to all of us:

THE MENTAL (THE POWER OF MIND-SET)

- Flexibility: adjustable focus and style
- Intentionality: mindful communication practices

THE EMOTIONAL (THE POWER OF FEELINGS)

- Emotional Intelligence: regulation and effective use of emotion
- Realness (authenticity): blending stoicism with humility and vulnerability

THE SOMATIC (THE POWER OF THE BODY)

- Collaboration: using proven methods to coach, mentor, and empower
- Engagement: managing the energy of work spaces to optimize teamwork, creativity, and performance

As part of the leadership team at the Institute of Coaching, an affiliate of McLean Hospital at Harvard Medical School, I make it my goal to conduct useful studies and read as much of the evidence-based research on trends in coaching and leadership as possible. As a coach for fast-growing companies such as Blue Apron and stalwarts including Morgan Stanley, I've focused on studies that can be easily understood and quickly implemented, and consolidated them into an accessible format for practical use by my clients—and now, you. It feels a little like giving away the store to say this, but it's true: You can be your own leadership coach.

Applying the Coach Approach

The goal of coaching is to support a client to change—and grow. Typically, I am asked to come in to work with an executive after she has been given feedback and discovered a misalignment between how she perceives herself and how she is perceived by others. We all have blind spots. Ironically, they emerge most often in the wake of success, not failure. It is often the things that we do well and with regularity— habits—that initially catapult us to promotion or recognition.

If you are great at details and always have the answer at your fingertips when the boss calls, you'll soon be the office expert. All well and good until that same boss says, "Love that you can give a ten-minute soliloquy in answer to every question, but I'm noticing that your tendency to dive into the minutiae with senior management doesn't always go over the way you would like. You need to learn to get to the point, or they may think you're not quite ready for a senior role." Ta-da. Blind spot revealed.

When I end up with a client in this or a similar situation, he often starts off with a deeply emotional sigh: "And here I am thinking that I'm doing great. At least that's what everyone told me until now. For so long I was the go-to guy for details, and now I'm too long-winded. Feels like I can't win." Yup—there's the wake-up call. It's called leadership development and it lies at the heart of coaching—recognizing your blind spots, getting clear on your strengths, and identifying the growing edge: What do you need to let go of? What do you need to expand on? How can you fulfill the apparent conundrum of pleasing everyone you lead and work for—without becoming a people pleaser?

Coaching is a support structure—call it a mirror or sounding board—that allows you to tackle yourself head-on, warts and all. All good coaches work with the science behind changing habits, helping clients raise their self-awareness, identify goals, choose and implement practices, and track progress. And celebrate wins! Progress on any kind of learning trajectory requires positive reinforcement; you've got to honor your successes.

As we begin this journey together, here's a basic rundown of the steps to coaching yourself:

1. **Identify the habit or behavior you want to change.** If you get feedback that you tend to be a bit authoritarian in your style, and you want to become a better listener or more democratic—to learn to build consensus instead of always dictating—it's time to start exploring how, when, where, and why the pattern has developed. You may find yourself feeling a bit defensive: "I tend to be directive because it is faster! I tend to make quick decisions because too much deliberation slows us down!" Watch out for that voice. We are not eliminating flaws, but expanding your repertoire of responses.
2. **Identify triggers.** All of our habitual behaviors are activated by a trigger point. Some are big moments, such as when the boss asks you to change direction—to save money, for instance—but most are smaller. Here's a classic example: Mary comes into Joe's office and tells him that one of her staff members is having a conflict with a teammate. Joe, a well-intentioned but extremely busy boss, absorbed with his buzzing phone, barely looks up from a desk piled high with paperwork. His immediate reaction: "Tell them to work it out . . . or else." Mary walks out feeling unsupported and dejected, and Joe feels temporarily relieved

from having to face the situation—but definitely hasn't alleviated the problem. This is where our core habits gets us in trouble, and where self-awareness, flexibility, and building positive habits can make all the difference.

3. **Identify the goal for change and the motivation behind it.** We all know that just *wanting* to be a better listener, to be more empathetic, or just to get more sleep, doesn't actually get us there. These thoughts tend to come and go, until they are out of sight and out of mind. The research clearly indicates that motivation, an intrinsic *why,* is key to action. So, before you decide to move the needle, explore the underlying reason you are doing it. Be clear on how this change will benefit not only your boss or your colleagues or your spouse, but you. Real motivation—the thing that gets us up earlier, eating better, walking more, listening more—comes from within, and requires a distinct picture of what the benefits will bring. Once my client Joe got beyond his frustration about being told to change how he communicated, he realized that he not only wanted to make his boss happy (extrinsic motivation), he wanted to become a mentor and role model for his staff (intrinsic motivation). He reconsidered his interactions with Mary and her colleagues. What could he have done differently? How could he shift gears in the moment, and respond with empathy to set the stage for a positive outcome?

4. **Start small with customized practices.** Numerous studies show that incremental improvements based on regular practice are key to success. True change takes time, starts small, and requires fostering habits that you don't dread. The truth is, if you consider a new practice "good for you" but basically a waste of time, you will quickly lose steam and revert to the old pattern that you

know and love. It's time to find practices that you want to do and come to associate with feeling great and making progress.

5. **Celebrate wins.** We are like dogs; rewards work. Far too often we make a change in the way we show up—we lead a meeting differently or add a fresh twist to our communication style—and no one appears to notice. That's where having a coach is incredibly valuable, because it is part of their job to remind you how far you've come and to celebrate each small success. But you don't *have* to have a coach to cheer your progress, if you can develop the habit of doing it yourself. It can be as simple as toasting the victory of a presentation or the fact that you went to yoga for the first time in a year. You did it, and that's awesome. If you celebrate, you just might keep it up!

In the following chapters, you will gain an insider's view on the real-life journeys, travails, and triumphs of leaders just like you. My goal is to provide you with examples, not just of famous corporate CEOs, but of leaders of all stripes and ages who are quietly revolutionizing how leadership works from the bottom up and the middle out. I share the latest scientific advances, along with coaching practices that can help you uncover and expand strengths, address blind spots, and learn to succeed where it matters most. I have designed the FIERCE model to be your leadership accelerator—to help you learn to *Flex*. It's time to jump-start your professional journey, to expand your skills, increase your impact, and elevate your life satisfaction. This model will help you thrive as a leader—wherever you are.

CHAPTER 1

Prep Work:
The Journey to Self-Awareness

"I was out of the office for only one day, and now it feels like my whole world is crashing down." Choking back tears, Barbara was unaware that she had just joined a storied lineage of what we might call the "oppressed leader," one whose blind spots had led, in her temporary absence, to a mild insurrection. A young project manager at a pharmaceutical research firm, Barbara had a team of eight project coordinators—each responsible for tracking a different set of clinical trials—who had approached her boss, the director of research, to complain about her behavior. She was accused of being impatient, critical, and, at times, harsh with feedback to the point where morale was low—and many on the team felt dejected and unmotivated.

If anyone was going to be fired, Barbara knew it wouldn't be the aggrieved workers. She admitted to me that under stress she did occasionally lash out at what she considered their immaturity and lack of follow-through. She knew better than to shout at them in the hallway, but every so often, she snapped.

Welcome to the brave new world of feedback. Barbara's moment under the microscope is hardly rare. Leadership is a journey, and that journey moves in the right direction only with a quality that we all spend a lifetime acquiring: self-awareness.

During my opening lecture for my NYU graduate-level leadership class, I ask, "How many of you consider yourselves to be self-aware?" On day one, trying to impress the teacher, three-quarters of the students raise their hands. Once I introduce the concept of EQ using Daniel Goleman's framework from his book, *Emotional Intelligence*, of self-awareness, self-management, social awareness, and relationship management, I ask them about the moments when they received the sting (or bolster) of feedback. How do they come to know their own talents, interests, and tendencies? Are they aware of how they are viewed by others?

This dialogue creates an interesting shift in the energy of the classroom, often bringing the students to a place of vulnerability and reflection. They tend to flip from overconfidence to self-effacement. When I wrap up by asking, "How many of you still consider yourselves to be self-aware?" there are few hands in the air, the students awake now to the hard truth that self-awareness is a lifelong journey along two interwoven paths: knowing yourself and knowing how others perceive you.

Ultimately, the most effective leaders develop both internal and external feedback practices that lead to greater alignment between how they see themselves and how the world sees them. When you know how you are perceived and you have a sense of your typical responses to the challenges and opportunities the world brings your way, you are more likely to feel grounded, centered, and energized—a solid foundation from which you can become agile as a leader.

Leadership Agility Self-Assessment

The Leadership Agility Self-Assessment will help you discover your own starting point for growth. Take a few minutes to read the questions in each of the six domains we will explore together. Then go back and, without overthinking—there is no right or wrong way to be—mark where you consider yourself to be on the spectrum from alpha to beta, or heroic to post-heroic, in your approach to each question.

FLEXIBLE

1. When making a decision do you tend to **declare** your position first or **explore** options with colleagues and vote?

2. Do you consider yourself adept at doing **multiple** activities at once, or do you prefer to **focus** on one activity at a time?

3. In a group setting, do you tend to **assert** your own vision and ideas, or prefer to **pull** ideas and input from others?

Authoritative	☐	☐	☐	☐	☐	☐	☐	☐	Consensus driven
Multitasker	☐	☐	☐	☐	☐	☐	☐	☐	Focused
Declarative	☐	☐	☐	☐	☐	☐	☐	☐	Inquisitive

INTENTIONAL

1. Is your **vision** of the future based on facts and data, or do you prefer stories that describe reality, speaking from "what's so" as a bridge to "what's possible"?

23

2. Do you motivate by sharing evidence and analysis, or do you prefer **aspirational communication** that connects through emotion?

3. Do you prefer to outline **goals and objectives** when declaring your intentions or to share the **meaning, purpose, and values** that underpin your goals?

Fact based	☐ ☐ ☐ ☐ ☐ ☐ ☐ ☐	Narrative driven
Analytical	☐ ☐ ☐ ☐ ☐ ☐ ☐ ☐	Aspirational
Strategic: "what"	☐ ☐ ☐ ☐ ☐ ☐ ☐ ☐	Meaningful: "why"

EMOTIONAL

1. Do you prefer to keep emotions, as much as possible, out of the work environment and focus on data, facts, and evidence? Or do you pay a lot of **attention to your feelings** and operate from gut instinct and intuition?

2. Do you downplay emotions and focus on the **rational aspects of decision-making,** or do you emphasize the need to **know your own feelings and connect** with how others feel?

3. Would you prefer to keep your emotions **in check,** or do you feel comfortable **expressing** emotions at work?

Data driven	☐	☐	☐	☐	☐	☐	☐	☐	Instinctive
Rational	☐	☐	☐	☐	☐	☐	☐	☐	Empathic
Reserved	☐	☐	☐	☐	☐	☐	☐	☐	Expressive

REAL

1. Do you see yourself as **self-assured and confident,** or as more **unassuming and humble?**

2. Do you tend to keep your **personal feelings to yourself,** or are you comfortable **sharing your values, beliefs, and idiosyncrasies?**

3. Do you prefer to lead from a **position of strength,** exuding power and confidence, or are you comfortable sharing your **humanness and vulnerability?**

Self-assured	☐	☐	☐	☐	☐	☐	☐	☐	Humble
Self-contained	☐	☐	☐	☐	☐	☐	☐	☐	Open
Strong	☐	☐	☐	☐	☐	☐	☐	☐	Vulnerable

COLLABORATIVE

1. Do you tend to be more **independent** within the organization, or do you **value working with others** to make decisions and move projects forward?

2. Do you **delegate**—give directions and set goals for others—or do you tend to **empower** colleagues and subordinates to figure out for themselves how they want to step up?

3. Do you enjoy **advising** people how to perform better based on your experience—or **engaging in coaching,** where people find their own way, with your support?

Independent	☐	☐	☐	☐	☐	☐	☐	☐	Interdependent
Delegating	☐	☐	☐	☐	☐	☐	☐	☐	Empowering
Advising	☐	☐	☐	☐	☐	☐	☐	☐	Coaching

ENGAGED

1. Are you driven more by the need for **results,** or do you prefer a more **fluid approach** that fosters new ideas and creativity?

2. Are you a **structured, disciplined** leader, or do you tend to "go with the flow," **comfortable with ambiguity** and a more flexible work environment?

3. Are you a **high-octane performer** who pushes yourself and others to perform, or do you prefer a **more relaxed** work environment with time for rest and reflection?

Productivity	☐	☐	☐	☐	☐	☐	☐	☐	Creativity
Structured	☐	☐	☐	☐	☐	☐	☐	☐	Fluid
High energy	☐	☐	☐	☐	☐	☐	☐	☐	Balanced energy

Now comes the part that requires a bit of courage: Share this assessment with a few of your colleagues. Ask them to reflect on the questions and mark a box, thinking about how they view your approach to each domain. Remind them that you are not trying to fit into any category, that there are no responses that are better or worse. Compare your initial reflections with theirs; where do you discover that others perceive you similarly or differently than you perceive yourself? Look for alignment and gaps. It is in the space between where we find opportunities for exploration and growth.

From Awareness to Action

Did you discover anything about yourself just in reflecting on the questions? How many of your peers gave you similar responses? Having used this assessment with hundreds of leaders, I find that the most common reaction is, "I rarely think about how I lead; I just do it." That's perfectly normal, of course. Yet, the benefits of reflection and feedback start to work their magic immediately. Once you have a sense of your natural baseline of behavior, fresh possibilities show up.

Analytical, exuberant, innovative, and passionate, Andrew had cofounded and steered an e-commerce start-up past its chaotic early days and remained in charge as the company prepared for an IPO. Early on, when survival was anything but assured, his habit of exuding strident confidence, barking orders, being impatient, moving fast, and instilling urgency were part of the recipe for success. But when I met him, two years later, his employees were on the verge of burnout. Suddenly, this same authoritative style was a liability. Andrew needed to flex. Not likely to ever become collegial, collaborative, or emotionally sensitive, he still needed to incorporate that beta behavior. Otherwise, he could very well lose the loyalty, support, and hard work of some of his best people.

Initially, Andrew just wanted his subordinates to undertake my assessment, but out of fairness, he agreed to submit to the same. He asked his direct reports, a few additional colleagues, and even his wife to fill out his evaluation. When I walked him through the results, he wasn't displeased or surprised; he was ranked as strongly alpha on most dimensions. He had to acknowledge, however, with the data in black-and-white, that many perceived him as being extremely directive and not particularly inquisitive. It was evident that although he was curious by nature, he had lost touch with effective listening habits in the rush for results.

I knew that Andrew had an analytical, cerebral orientation—he respected data—so I shared cutting-edge research and mixed in suggestions for a couple of new habits to consider. First, I showed him surveys conducted by Harvard, Duke's Fuqua School of Business, and other leadership consultancies on those attributes most admired in C-suite execs. The results were both a balm and a wake-up call. At the top of the list were big-picture vision (Andrew had this in spades), inspirational communication (he could summon it when needed), building cohesive teams (he faltered a bit here, but still considered this skill strong), and, finally, good listening and fostering an inclusive, creative culture. "Well, three out of five is not so bad," he joked. But he got the point: Executives who listen well and pay attention to culture come out on top. What could Andrew do to better interact with his staff? I offered him these suggestions:

1. Ask more open-ended questions, instead of posing "yes" or "no" questions, which tend to shut down the conversation, and make time—even just a pause—to hear people out.

2. Pay attention to pronouns, using "we" and "our" instead of declarations that start with "I" or "my," which tend to put you on a pedestal and create distance between you and your team.

3. When it's time for a check-in, get out of your office and meet people in a neutral space. Take five to ten minutes for listening—real listening. People need time and space, and if you want to know what's going on in the business, you must create room for both. When you call people into your office and demand an update, your staff will comply—and learn to tell you exactly what you want to hear, in five minutes or less.

Like many leaders, Andrew tended to default to "I," which was great for sending signals of command and competence. He was surprised to learn that something as simple as minding his pronouns would help. It wasn't a matter of right and wrong, but what worked. I encouraged him to assign a close confidant to give him regular feedback on how many times he used "we" versus "I" in group discussions.

Once Andrew had developed two simple habits—asking open-ended questions followed by time for listening, and speaking to groups using "we"—the entire tenor of the office began to shift. He developed a reputation for being more inclusive and team oriented. His company's cofounder even stopped me one day and whispered, "Jeff, what are you doing to Andrew? He seems so much more relaxed. Yesterday he sat through an hour-long meeting with us and didn't scream, didn't look at his phone, didn't get impatient or roll his eyes." I said I wasn't surprised: "Andrew has great leadership instincts. He just needs to expand his repertoire; that's often what most of us need."

Mental, Emotional, and Somatic Leaders

Research conducted at the University of Copenhagen on the way leaders influence and impact followers has shown that nonverbal interactions can encourage a positive or negative result as much or even more than a conversation itself. Researchers placed bio-mimicry sensors on leaders in a simulated work situation so that they could record the way different physical stances—leaning in or crossing their arms, looking away or directly at subordinates—impacted their colleagues' reactions while receiving feedback. It turned out that how they engaged nonverbally resulted in substantially different levels of receptivity. Those leaders whose body language was more open, relaxed, and connected—with eye contact, smiles, and even light touch at appropriate moments—had a much more positive outcome. Subordinates even reported that leaders whose bodily movements mirrored their own were better at giving feedback.

It may appear obvious that the physical stance with which you approach another person will impact their sense of connection, trust, and willingness to listen, but it's not always easy to keep in mind. When we want someone to pay attention, it helps to create a sense of safety, to connect with more than just words; gestures, eye contact, and facial expressions matter. In moments of stress, some people sit quietly and reflect, arms crossed, head bowed, while others will literally rise to the occasion, getting up and walking around, preferring to be in action mode. The science demonstrates that this somatic dimension of leadership may make all the difference. No matter how well intentioned your words and feelings, how you show up enhances the possibility of being heard—or shuts it down altogether.

I was asked by the CEO of a fast-growing start-up in online fashion merchandising to facilitate a two-hour brainstorming session with his two cofounders. Even though the company was doing well overall, revenues had been flat. The CEO was concerned that the downturn could have a deleterious effect on the morale of the entire company unless the founders acted to quell the noise and reinforce their positive long-term prospects. It turned out to be a grueling, tense session, where each of their styles—one a thinker, one a feeler, and one a doer—showed up in stark relief.

The chief executive officer, a consummate thinker, wanted to hold a town hall and put together a PowerPoint presentation with all the data demonstrating that the downturn was a mere blip in a bigger picture of success. The more emotive chief operating officer agreed to the town hall, but rather than a data-driven one, he lobbied for an open forum for dialogue to, as he put it, "give people an opportunity to vent, and make us all feel better." And, finally, the physically in-clined chief technology officer recommended that they take the entire corporate staff into the wilderness for a rafting or camping trip. He argued that, instead of pontificating on the numbers, which everyone was sick to death of hearing about, and, instead of holding a "Kumbaya hug fest," it would help morale more to get everyone out of the office and let them work off their anxieties doing something active and fun.

Ultimately, they decided to hold a town hall and present figures demonstrating that the business situation would soon improve, then host an open forum, and finally devote a Friday for a barbecue and baseball game. This may be an extreme example, but you can see how a leader's natural tendencies often result in behavior that can have a big impact. Can you also see that, depending upon their followers, any one of these approaches could work well or be disastrous? These guys covered their bases, but we don't always have the time nor the luxury to try multiple techniques, which is why it can be very helpful for a leader to be aware of their default style. It is also key to keep in mind that you may need to modify, adjust, and even hold back from what comes naturally to address the needs of subordinates or colleagues.

When Brad, the extroverted and high-energy CTO just mentioned, took the Leadership Energy Self-Assessment (on the next page), and discovered that he was a somatic leader, it was a revelation. Always having seen himself as a bit of a geek engineer, he had never noticed that his tendency under stress was to always be in motion. He had thought that his frustration with more cerebral colleagues was simple impatience, and hadn't recognized that his love of high-energy activities was a key source of creative energy both for himself and his team. His desire to get everyone together in an active setting turned out to be the spark that his high-functioning engineers needed to keep the ideas flowing.

It was also important for Brad to recognize the need to slow down at times, to be reflective and thoughtful about his decision-making and communication styles, both of which require a focused mind-set. Great motivators learn how to step back and read their audience—not everyone wants to run out and play volleyball or make major decisions during a shouting match. Some folks appreciate a decisive management style, while others prefer to be included in decisions or feel more motivated by data or a well-crafted story line delivered with sobriety and deliberation. Knowing how to switch gears and adjust to the group dynamic requires flexibility along with clear and intentional communication—and these, as we will explore in the next two chapters, are the natural domains of the cerebral leader. Brad ultimately mastered these approaches as well, but first he had to become aware of his habits—and their strengths and liabilities—and be willing to adjust.

Spend a few minutes on the following self-assessment to determine where you tend to focus your energy.

Leadership Energy Self-Assessment

Go through the items below and reflect on how you normally think, feel, and operate in the world. Mark "T" for the items that resonate. Mark "F" for the items that do not typically apply. There is no right or wrong way to score this diagnostic. When you have completed the list, add up the total number of true answers and determine the percentage that apply to you by dividing the total number by 30.

CEREBRAL TYPE: THINKER

1. Enjoys analyzing and dissecting subjects ☐ T ☐ F

2. Enjoys rhetorical conversation ☐ T ☐ F

3. Thinks in hypotheses, frameworks, and models ☐ T ☐ F

4. Decides using logic and analysis ☐ T ☐ F

5. Tends to respect the rational argument ☐ T ☐ F

6. Expresses feelings as thoughts ☐ T ☐ F

7. Likes facts and data ☐ T ☐ F

8. Enjoys studying and research ☐ T ☐ F

9. Enjoys reading nonfiction ☐ T ☐ F

10. Respects intellectual rigor and debate ☐ T ☐ F

11. Expresses compassion with logic ☐ T ☐ F

12. Head-centered in approach to life ☐ T ☐ F

13. Experiences concrete visions and fantasies ☐ T ☐ F

14. Enjoys brainstorming ☐ T ☐ F

15. Enjoys solving problems ☐ T ☐ F

16. Likes to dissect ideas ☐ T ☐ F

17. Always wants to have more information ☐ T ☐ F

18. Tends to enjoy technology, computers, gadgets ☐ T ☐ F

19. Writes in an organized, thoughtful fashion ☐ T ☐ F

20. Enjoys political discourse ☐ T ☐ F

21. Tends to ruminate, philosophize ☐ T ☐ F

22. May procrastinate by getting caught up
    in planning ☐ T ☐ F

23. Fear expresses as depression, boredom ☐ T ☐ F

24. Thinks before acting □ T □ F

25. Motto: Let me think about it □ T □ F

26. Can be overwhelmed with data □ T □ F

27. Fear mode: frozen then fight/flight □ T □ F

28. Tends to daydream rather than night dream □ T □ F

29. Insights and intuitions come in words,
    thoughts, ideas □ T □ F

30. Meditation challenge: quieting the mind □ T □ F

Total number of "T," or true, answers: _____
Percentage of true answers (total number divided by 30,
then multiplied by 100): _____

EMPATHIC TYPE: FEELER

1. Expresses feelings directly □ T □ F

2. Decides with the heart □ T □ F

3. Drawn to images more than words □ T □ F

4. Appreciates subjective reality more
   than scientific fact □ T □ F

5. Expresses feelings with compassion/empathy ☐ T ☐ F

6. Values relationships more than ideas ☐ T ☐ F

7. Wants to feel passionate and engaged
   with people, not things ☐ T ☐ F

8. Can be mercurial, melodramatic ☐ T ☐ F

9. Debates with passion rather than logic ☐ T ☐ F

10. Focuses on the pain of others ☐ T ☐ F

11. May have bouts of guilt or self-doubt ☐ T ☐ F

12. May have difficulties maintaining
    personal boundaries ☐ T ☐ F

13. Tends to have vivid, colorful night dreams ☐ T ☐ F

14. Enjoys reading fiction and/or poetry ☐ T ☐ F

15. Loves music over silence ☐ T ☐ F

16. Can be overwhelmed by emotions ☐ T ☐ F

17. Procrastination tends to become drama ☐ T ☐ F

18. Tends to love the arts over sports ☐ T ☐ F

19. Writes in metaphor; uses analogies   □ T □ F

20. Loves stories and narrative   □ T □ F

21. Can be dismissive of logic   □ T □ F

22. Heart-centered in approach to life   □ T □ F

23. Fear expresses as anger, sadness   □ T □ F

24. Can feel overwhelmed at times   □ T □ F

25. Loves just being in nature   □ T □ F

26. Fear mode: flight not fight   □ T □ F

27. Needs a great deal of rest/sleep   □ T □ F

28. Insights show up in pictures/images   □ T □ F

29. Can appear indecisive or wishy-washy   □ T □ F

30. Meditation challenge: not being swept away
    by emotions   □ T □ F

Total number of "T," or true, answers: _____
Percentage of true answers (total number divided by 30,
then multiplied by 100): _____

SOMATIC TYPE: DOER

1. Prefers practicing over theorizing ☐ T ☐ F

2. Enjoys conversation while moving ☐ T ☐ F

3. May avoid reading or writing ☐ T ☐ F

4. Results oriented; may be impatient
   with procrastinators ☐ T ☐ F

5. Practical and pragmatic ☐ T ☐ F

6. Needs to have concrete goals ☐ T ☐ F

7. Appreciates multitasking ☐ T ☐ F

8. Prefers physical exercise over contemplation ☐ T ☐ F

9. Likes to build things or take things apart ☐ T ☐ F

10. Can become overwhelmed with activity ☐ T ☐ F

11. Enjoys physical activities, athletics, sports ☐ T ☐ F

12. Tends to be group oriented, avoiding solitude ☐ T ☐ F

13. Enjoys nature for hiking, movement, exploration ☐ T ☐ F

14. Respects physical prowess, strength ☐ T ☐ F

15. Communicates in short bursts   □ T □ F

16. Tends to focus on logistics, action items   □ T □ F

17. Prefers making music more than listening   □ T □ F

18. Loves to watch sports, contests   □ T □ F

19. Loves active creative hobbies: cooking, pottery, knitting   □ T □ F

20. Loves competition   □ T □ F

21. Fear mode: fight not flight   □ T □ F

22. Tends to ignore or dismiss physical ailments   □ T □ F

23. Prefers to work with hands   □ T □ F

24. Can be reactive, aggressive   □ T □ F

25. Tends to be in constant motion   □ T □ F

26. Fear expresses through over-functioning, anxiety   □ T □ F

27. Tends to be dismissive of depression   □ T □ F

28. May not sleep enough   □ T □ F

29. Intuits through the core: respects gut reaction ☐ T ☐ F

30. Meditation challenge: sitting still ☐ T ☐ F

Total number of "T," or true, answers: _____
Percentage of true answers (total number divided by 30,
then multiplied by 100): _____

There is no good or bad way to exert leadership energy, as there are mental, emotional, and somatic components to every move we make. By adding up your true answers, dividing by 30, and then multiplying the result by 100, you can determine which of the three tendencies tends to be your default. It could be that you're well balanced in all three, but most of us have one area that is dominant. Recognizing an affinity for one over another is helpful in raising your awareness of how you may react to challenges, especially under stress. That can free you up to consider your options, be aware of how others may operate differently, and help you stretch out of your comfort zone.

PART I

Mental Leadership

CHAPTER 2

A Mind-set for Mastery

When I met Uri, he was sitting alone in a dark office in a high-rise where all the private offices are on the inside, and cubicles ring the perimeter. Instead of a window, floor-to-ceiling glass walls looked out over the cubes where his team worked, which might have been fine had his colleagues not sauntered by at regular intervals, glancing in at us with a look of disdain that caused Uri to cringe. I was immediately struck by the oppressive heat. I had no idea how long Uri had been sitting by himself, waiting patiently, as I was a few minutes late, but he was sweating profusely, his brow furrowed and droplets of sweat nestling between the lines on his forehead.

Withdrawn, sullen, and obviously depressed at the mere notion that he was to have a coach, Uri may have been dripping with sweat on the outside, but he was dried up and parched on the inside. I worried that we were doomed to fail. I also knew that the feedback from his subordinates, many of whom sat a few short feet from us outside the wall of glass, was not pretty. But his boss told me that he was supportive of Uri and had faith that he could change.

In his early thirties, Uri was a software engineer who had come to the United States via Israel and Germany. He had moved his young family to New York City two years before and quickly became a rising star. In many aspects of his technical job, he was brilliant. But his style—assertive, ambitious, driven, and direct—had alienated his colleagues, to the point where three of them had requested his removal. They described him as pushy, impatient, controlling, and dictatorial. I knew that someone with his talent—with the right mind-set—could integrate feedback and develop a more sensitive leadership style.

But after three sessions, I came to dread our overheated late-afternoon meetings. Uri deflected and denied that he had any culpability for the low morale of his team. He would go on long rants about how they were lazy, incompetent, whiny, and immature—that if only he were a director he could hire the "right" people and weed out the losers. He was also extremely resistant to taking his boss's feedback seriously, and was always quick with an excuse about the political motivations behind any perceived criticism.

I knew that if he didn't trust his team, a feedback exercise with them would be a waste of time, and a potential disaster. Instead, I suggested that he fill out the Leadership Agility Self-Assessment (see chapter 1), but only with the goal of helping him reflect on his personal style. To Uri, this sounded reasonable. For me, it provided a slight opening.

A week later, I started our session by asking Uri how he was feeling about the coaching. Suddenly this confident, assertive, even brash former army sergeant had tears in his eyes. This startling moment of vulnerability gave me goose bumps. "What's going on?" I said. "You seem upset."

Uri explained haltingly that at dinner the night before he had casually shared the assessment with his wife. Later, Uri overheard their ten-year-old son asking what she was reading. She told him that she was helping Daddy with a training program that he was doing at work. Their son asked, "Is this gonna help Daddy be nicer?"

She responded, "Well, I don't know if he'll be nicer, but hopefully this training will help him be a better boss. He wants to get promoted."

Their son whispered, "No wonder he needs training. Dad is not very nice. He is always bossy. He's always giving me a hard time. He's never supportive. Nothing is ever good enough for Dad. I'm not surprised he needs help at work."

Uri was aghast. It never dawned on him that the way he interacted with his children would have any correlation to the way he operated at work. He later asked his wife what she thought, to which she replied, "Well, you are tough on the kids. There have been many times when the little one has run to me in tears because you run out of patience and yell. You never fail to let them know that you're disappointed. Sometimes they're just scared of you."

I could feel that something had shifted deep in his soul. The feedback that had been swirling between us for weeks was finally hitting home. A ten-year-old boy who was afraid of his own father was the wake-up call that Uri could finally hear. His heartfelt sorrow was soon replaced by a newfound lightness that crossed his face. I knew that he would never be the same. Feedback, when you are ready to hear it, is powerful.

Over the next months, we worked together at a rapid pace. He quickly came to understand that being assertive, smart, analytical, hardworking, and demanding, although all admirable qualities, needed to be complemented with listening, sensitivity to others, and empathy. As his trust in himself—and me—deepened to another level of vulnerability, he mentioned that he had always "loved" his fellow soldiers. Uri was deeply sensitive and caring, but had decided somewhere along the way that being soft or compassionate was akin to being weak. Of course, nothing could be further from the truth. His brittle attitude was the one thing in the way of his growth.

Uri has gone on to become a senior vice president at his firm and regularly checks in with me to, as he would put it, "test his mind-set." It is experiences like this one that foster my love of coaching, but, more important, my belief that we can all wake up at any moment and shift our perspective, opening ourselves to the gift of feedback.

As we navigate how to effectively lead in today's topsy-turvy landscape, I want to share three science-based theoretical underpinnings that you can fall back on—even when you falter, resist, or find yourself drowning in the sea of change: 1. reframing feedback; 2. positive psychology's PERMA model; and 3. developing a growth mind-set.

1. Feedforward Instead of Feedback

Typically, feedback involves something like asking colleagues to report their experience with a client based on past behaviors. World-renowned coach Marshall Goldsmith suggests we instead move toward what he calls "feedforward." Feedforward shifts the onus away from having others assess your weaknesses, instead asking you to reflect on what you might want to change or improve. Before you receive feedback, if you're thinking about opportunities for expanding what you do well, then you're already on track to seeing yourself as a work in progress.

First, think about one thing you'd like to be better at or one thing that you see others doing particularly well and would love to emulate.

Second, ask someone you trust: What could I do to improve in this area? Rather than asking what you've done in the past that may or may not have worked, channel your energy toward changing something tomorrow. If you want to improve the way you present in meetings, Marshall suggests approaching a colleague who has seen you give a presentation, and asking, "Could you share with me one thing that I could do differently?" Then ask them if they'd be willing to support you by observing you in action—and providing pointers. Or look around for a role model who does it well, and approach them for advice. And always have what I call a "celebration strategy" so that you remember to take time to revel in the small steps you take toward mastery. When you ask confidants for continued feedforward, have them tell you what is working, no matter how small—and find ways to celebrate your progress.

Neuroscience has demonstrated that one of the reasons receiving feedback is so daunting is that our brains are wired to be on guard for input that undermines our sense of self. After thousands of years of development in an untamed world where life-threatening predators lurked around every corner, the brain is acutely tuned in to anything that threatens our sense of safety and security. And when it comes these days—more likely in the boardroom than on the savannah—it can trigger our fight-or-flight response.[1]

2. Positive Psychology's PERMA Model

A second framework that I employ with clients who are struggling with a negative outlook comes from Marty Seligman and his colleagues at the University of Pennsylvania, who conducted many studies asking variations of "What makes humans thrive?" This research showed that fostering an energy around what works instead of what's missing tends to open our minds to change and growth. The studies led to a framework of five core elements of human behavior that underpin our psychological well-being. Incorporate each into your mind-set, and you are much more likely to live, and lead, from a place of optimism, happiness, and meaning.

- **Positive Emotion:** Experiencing positive feelings—awe, joy, gratitude, love, and the like—has a direct connection to thriving. Focusing on the positive and not dwelling on the negative helps us to view the past, present, and future with greater perspective and optimism. It also inspires us to be more creative, more curious, and more willing to try new things. Even when negative life events occur, such as illness, accidents, and economic downturns, shifting our focus toward the positive brings us more quickly out of the downward spiral that can lead to depression.[2]
- **Engagement:** Whether it's playing an instrument, working out, or diving into a project, studies demonstrate that in moments of deep engagement, time tends to feel suspended or slowed down, and a blissful sense of what scientist Mihaly Csikszentmihalyi calls "flow"—an intense sense of focus—emerges. This state of bliss has traditionally been considered a sign of genius or divine intervention. Today we know that it is both, and more: Flow is achievable by us ordinary mortals (who all have a touch of genius within us) just by taking time to discover what we love to do and fostering it. When you focus on what most interests you, honoring your innate curiosity, work becomes play—something you do with pleasure, joy, and a sense of purpose. Finding a place for flow in your life is key to building the self-awareness and self-confidence to stretch your intelligence, skills, and emotional capabilities.

- **Relationships:** As social animals, we thrive on strong emotional and physical interactions.[3] Building positive connections with your parents, siblings, peers, and friends is important, and since we spend a large portion of our lives at work, the same is true for workplace relationships. We all know how debilitating it can be to have unpleasant or conflicted relationships with colleagues. In fact, studies have shown that workplace relationships, because of their direct impact on our economic security, can be more essential to thriving than our home lives. Leaders I coach often get caught up in the transactional nature of work relationships and either ignore or dismiss the value of friendship and belonging. They do so at their peril.

- **Meaning:** Research has shown that people who have a sense of purpose and meaning in their lives tend to be healthier and happier. In a world where pleasure and wealth are often touted as the keys to the castle, most of us recognize that while material success can provide temporary feelings of security, true fulfillment emanates from a deeper place. That's why even though I believe anyone can become an effective leader, those who take the time to reflect on *why* they want to lead, exploring what being a leader means to them at an emotional level beyond beating the competition or making the next pay grade, are the most likely to prosper. Those who connect their aspiration with a cause bigger than themselves—who, as trite as it may sound, want to make a difference—are more likely to coach themselves, and be open to coaching from others, to develop the fortitude and resilience to overcome whatever challenges come their way.

- **Accomplishments:** One of the most common situations that I see with clients who become insecure in the face of a new experience (whether it's starting a new job, taking a risk on a project, or even launching a new business) is how quick they are to dismiss, deny, or seemingly forget about their past achievements. Studies of highly successful people indicate that the key to staying motivated is developing an awareness of, and a sense of gratitude for, their accomplishments. Being able to reflect on our triumphs when the going gets tough has a salutary and motivating effect, helping us overcome setbacks that come our way.[4]

Intrinsic motivation is a tricky mechanism, and even paradoxical, as some parts of our brain are wired to seek equilibrium and resist change—with the intention of keeping us safe and comfortable—while other brain functions seek novelty, relish competition, and energize us to take risks, strive, and grow. It is difficult to make change happen if your primary focus is on what is broken or not working. Instead, identify your strengths. This is one of the primary reasons why the leadership agility assessment you completed does not judge alpha or beta attributes as better or worse, because depending upon the context, either can be effective. The organizational landscape may be evolving to include more space for beta-style leadership, as I discussed earlier, but that will not negate the importance of alpha talents; it just expands and includes them.

3. Get Yourself a Growth Mind-set

When I first met Xavier, he was an executive search consultant at a major firm with a strong reputation with his clients. Still in his early thirties, he had accomplished much of what he had set out to do after graduating with an advanced business degree from a top university in France, but he was miserable. The thing is, Xavier had always wanted to be an artist.

With a passion for abstract painting, drawing, and multidimensional art, Xavier had kept his dream alive with an endless array of projects on which he spent much of his free time. His apartment was overflowing with paintings, sculptures, and huge unfinished canvases. When he hired me, we ostensibly were going to work on getting him a promotion to partner, but I knew from the outset that his heart lay elsewhere. But even as I sat in an apartment overflowing with the work of an artist, his mind was totally fixed in the belief that he was not an artist.

I remember asking Xavier, "How can you not consider yourself an artist when you spend almost all your nonwork time making art?"

He replied, "I know I have an artistic nature, Jeff, and love art. But I'm not really an artist. I could never make a living with art. I'll always be a dabbler."

The final framework that I use with clients who are caught up in a negative or limiting self-concept is inspired by the work of Stanford University psychologist and researcher Carol Dweck, who wrote the enormously successful book *Mindset* based on her research into the distinction between "fixed" and "growth" mind-sets. After studying the classroom environments and teaching techniques used with young children over many years, she concluded that children who are most likely to succeed exhibit a growth mind-set—an ability to learn from mistakes, stay motivated in the face of setbacks, and maintain a consistent level of motivation. Children with a fixed mind-set, on the other hand, even when they have a great deal of potential as indicated by IQ and aptitude tests, are more likely to get stuck, lose momentum, or become demotivated in the wake of mistakes or small setbacks.

Just providing praise, or telling a child that they are talented, is not enough to promote a growth mind-set; it may, in fact, reinforce the opposite. Children who are told they are "smart" often come to expect learning to be easy. When it is difficult, they struggle to stay engaged. On the other hand, children who are given feedback focused not so much on who they "are" but on how they are evolving and learning tend to develop a view of themselves as capable but not overconfident.[5]

Telling Xavier that, from what I could observe, he was already an artist didn't have any impact. His mind-set wasn't just fixed; it was entrenched. He held firm to the belief that a "true" artist would be showing in a gallery and making a living through their work. My job was not so much to talk him out of this mind-set, but challenge his beliefs and assist him in replacing his either-or inner dialogue— whether he was or wasn't an artist—with a both-and perspective.

"Don't worry so much about whether you are an artist or not," I told him. "Just commit more time to your hobby—expand your scheduled time for art projects, share your excitement about art and your work with colleagues, bring a few paintings into the office." Xavier's shift in mind-set was gradual. He asked colleagues to come see a few of his pieces, but still loudly declared that it was just a sideshow. I didn't try to build up his self-esteem or convince him that he was talented. I focused instead on getting him to target his energy on what he enjoyed, what provided meaning and purpose: the work.

Soon enough, he showed up at a session glowing with a sense of accomplishment: a colleague had not only purchased one of his paintings, she had offered to hold a show for him in the lobby of their office building! "Yikes," he said to me, a bit red in the face with excitement. "I guess I have to 'come out' as an artist now." Soon he started networking and showing his work to the world—which led to public exposure and ultimately large commissions. Through it all, his mind continued to conduct debates on whether he was legit, but he eventually learned to follow his heart and keep his body in action, doing the work.

Jump ahead five years and Xavier has done a 180. He now calls himself an artist who dabbles in recruiting. Xavier was always destined to be a successful artist—and a successful businessperson—because he had the work ethic, energy, and commitment to be both. My only job was to be a mirror for him to see how he was holding himself back, to help him rewire his mental framework to unleash those abundant capacities that were just waiting to come forth. Can you do the same?

Are You Ready to Grow?

These evidence-based foundations are designed to help you frame your development as a leader from the reference point of what's possible, *not* what's wrong. As you continue to explore your decision-making and communication styles in the next chapters, reflect on the mind-set you are bringing. If you find yourself shutting down and thinking "I don't need to worry about that" or "This doesn't apply to me," stop and ask yourself, "What might I be resisting?" As we will explore in later chapters, even the tiniest triggers—irritants or pet peeves—often signify an opportunity to reflect on your mind-set and ask, "Am I open, flexible, and growing?"

CHAPTER 3

Be Flexible:
From Alpha to Beta and Back

Sitting on the sofa in a cramped office in a large academic medical center in Boston, I waited patiently for my first meeting with Magda. She was twenty minutes late—which, I learned later, was pretty much the norm. I had been warned that she was a "tough cookie" and "headstrong." The senior leaders who had recommended she join my leadership development program had all spoken highly of her intellect and her passion for work and patients but were also critical of her style. As her boss put it, "Magda is one of the best doctors we have, but she is still early in her career and needs to slow down and be more willing to take direction, be less intense with the staff. We love her, but she doesn't seem to understand that in an ancient academic institution like this one, big changes take time; decisions don't happen just by the force of her will. She will need to step back and be a better team player if she hopes to grow into a top leader here."

When she did come flying in to greet me, I was taken aback. Friendly, soft-spoken, apologetic for being late, she pulled a chair away from her desk and put it right in front of me, so we were eye-to-eye. I found myself across from one of the nicest, most attentive and open people I would ever meet. She was "thrilled," as she put it, to be working with a coach. She knew that her hard-driving style was frustrating her boss. She knew that she worked harder and faster and with more passion than many of her colleagues. But she wasn't in the least bit full of herself. On the contrary, she was deeply aware that her tendency to push hard for improvements and willingness to change things up—no matter whose feathers she ruffled—was getting her in hot water with some higher-ups.

Given that Magda was already a successful supervisor and was interested in developing herself as a leader, I knew she had that one quality that makes all the difference: a mind-set for mastery. She was open to feedback, aware of the fact that she sometimes rubbed people the wrong way, and wanted to grow. Rather than starting from the assumption that there was anything wrong, I asked Magda to share what she considered to be her top five strengths. She told me she thought of herself as creative, hardworking, persistent, passionate, and analytical. The next step was to look at whether there might be a downside to any of these strengths. For example, I asked her, "Can you think of a situation where being persistent or passionate could be a barrier to your success?"

I already knew from speaking to her boss, Tim, that one of his frustrations was Magda's lack of patience and reluctance to work through the "chain of command." Rather than me just passing along this feedback, which she might dismiss as one more example of her boss trying to hold her back, it would be more valuable for her to come to this conclusion herself. "Well, I have on occasion just gone ahead and set up a meeting with another department chair, without notifying Tim first. But it's not because I want to go around Tim; it's because I'm committed to getting things done." Bingo. It didn't take much else to have Magda see how her passion for progress could trip her up in the political arena.

In many ways, Magda is a classic alpha leader. The strengths that she knew about herself had been cultivated over many years, as a top student in Varanasi, India, when she was a child, and while achieving high marks in medical school, pursuing postgraduate studies and a clinical fellowship in the United States, and ultimately landing at Harvard and a fast-track career. She had learned to be assertive, even authoritative, to stand out in environments where being a woman, and a foreigner, might have put her at the back of the line.

I see it all the time: Our strengths, sometimes the very talents we are most applauded for, can suddenly become obstacles to our next level of success. When we do something well, we tend to continue to do it; the world rewards us, and it becomes a habit. But when the situation changes, and our responsibilities and accountabilities change, that very same capability no longer serves us.

Likewise, our perceptions of ourselves must continually evolve and broaden, necessitating a letting-go process. We must leave behind limiting beliefs such as "I am independent and can go it alone." Magda didn't need to tamp down her passion or work ethic, but she did need to see how driving toward results without asking for support or bringing others along could limit her ability to navigate an entrenched bureaucracy, or knock her agenda out of alignment with her peers'.

One of the challenges Magda was running up against was the fact that her boss, an alpha himself, had a similar style, so there was a natural tension between them. And as much as he respected her ability to get things done, he was often frustrated with her reluctance, in his appraisal, to take direction and be patient with the politics inherent at a large institution.

I frequently encounter leaders who have developed a fixed mind-set, a way of habitually seeing themselves, and who are completely unaware of two stumbling blocks to their success: 1. Your default style works only until it doesn't; 2. Your default style creates a perception by others that this is "who you are"—so even if you adapt with a new mind-set, many will not be persuaded.

For Magda, cultivating a more flexible leadership style involved expanding her repertoire of competencies to include three key attributes, all of which she had the ability to do well but had spent less time and energy practicing: 1. being patient and listening; 2. slowing down and focusing; and 3. leveraging her natural curiosity to bring out the best in others. If you happened to fall more toward the alpha side of the spectrum on the Leadership Agility Self-Assessment, these attributes may very well be your Achilles' heel as well.

Becoming a Better Listener

Before jumping into specific practices, it helps to dispel some of the myths about listening. It's a truism that there are two types of listening: active and passive. I'm not sure how this dichotomy got traction, because all true listening is active. If you're "passively listening," you're probably distracted, attempting to multitask, or just not paying attention. Put simply: You are not listening.

Some coaches also speak about different levels of listening, most often describing them as a hierarchy: At level one, you are listening to a speaker's words but are more focused on your own thoughts and responses. At level two, you focus on the other person's words, tone, and nonverbal expressions and shift the emphasis away from yourself. Level three is "global listening," in which you take in not only words and nonverbal expressions, but scan the environment for the emotional context, becoming aware of the energetic field that surrounds you both.

These distinctions can be useful, but are somewhat arbitrary and overly complex. As I said, all listening is active listening, and has two components: listening from the inside out, or listening from the outside in. "From the inside out"—what some people think of as level one—means paying attention to what's going on within yourself while listening to someone else. "From the outside in" refers to paying attention to the words, tone, pace, body language, and energy of the other party, while also taking in the environment around you. All effective listening involves the interplay between both.[1]

Here is the key question for agile leaders: How much should you speak versus listen if you want to both understand others deeply and be understood yourself? Some experts will say the ratio is 20/80, but the question itself is problematic. Connection and understanding between two people or a group doesn't have anything to do with the number of words spoken or the amount of speaking versus listening. It emerges from a neurological resonance process, which happens in nanoseconds, and is fundamentally an emotional response to a range of sensory signals—not just words. A smile, a hand gesture, or a pantomime can even lead to a better outcome. That said, if you're spending a high percentage of your time speaking, you're probably not truly listening. For a typical alpha leader, like Magda, less is more. But there is no magic ratio. What I find works best with clients instead is to focus on what I call the "three P's": presence, perspective, and persona.

1. Cultivate a Listening Presence
Start with this question: When having an important conversation, how much time do you spend planning what you are about to say and

how much time do you spend being present? The 20/80 ratio may not be a bad rule of thumb for an interview-style dialogue, but the real answer is this: It depends. We are always listening and we are also always talking, because we speak and listen with not just our ears but with our whole being. Our brains can process only one idea or concept or memory at a time, but our bodies are talented multitaskers: You receive and process signals from the physical expression, verbal tone, pace, and movements of your interlocutor simultaneously. You are likewise communicating with your face, eyes, gestures, and posture, and the tone, pitch, and pace of your speech. Core to becoming a good listener is paying attention to your physical expression, as well as noticing the nonverbal cues you send.

Magda reflected on these questions over a period of a few weeks, taking notes after key interactions. She came to see that her biggest challenge was her overarching desire to "get to the point." She had limited patience for small talk. At the same time, she realized the importance of building relationships, and came to see that so-called small talk, where the focus is personal or, better said, *interpersonal,* is where trust, intimacy, and connection are built.

With this in mind, she made up her own homework: She committed to spending quality time with key colleagues by taking at least one person out for a coffee each week. At first it didn't come naturally—but it worked. Magda's colleagues shifted their perception of her from workhorse ("Watch out, here she comes with more tasks for us to do") to colleague ("Hey, there's Magda, maybe I should stop and say hello"). She soon came to see that getting to know the people she worked with was invaluable when she wanted to get stuff done. It may seem obvious, but the habit of listening presence—in her case, attending to the person, not the task—made all the difference.

2. Become Aware of Your Listening Perspective

When was the last time you sat down for a conversation with a colleague, manager, or subordinate without having an agenda? If you are like most of us, you have meetings with a goal in mind, just as Magda did, every day. Even when she started hanging out with her colleagues for more personal, quality time, she still had a goal: to get to know them, feel more connected, and build a stronger foundation for future task-oriented interactions.

We all have what I call a "listening perspective." Just as we see the world through a specific lens, bringing our opinions and values to whatever is laid out before us, we do the same with listening. Not only do we have an agenda, whether we are aware of it or not; we also hear everything through the filter of our interests and beliefs. Far too often, we engage with others without thinking about how these cornerstones of our identity underpin our motivation. Far too often, what we call "listening" is more like a mild form of collusion where we seek to determine, "Is this person or group on my side? Are they for or against me?"

Are you aware of how your judgments may color the way you listen? Are you listening to hear the perspective of another person, or are you listening to have your own opinions validated?

To become an agile listener, Magda had to notice how her training as a physician, her cultural background, and her beliefs and opinions informed how she engaged with others. Our exploration led her to become aware that she had two underlying perspectives that she brought to almost every interaction. The first evolved directly out of her medical training: a tendency to listen and ask questions about what's "wrong" and what needs to be "fixed." For physicians, trained to diagnose problems and immediately determine solutions, this mind-set makes perfect sense. Second was her tendency to listen for symptoms, with a goal of alleviating pain; again, appropriate for a healer.

Within a leadership dynamic, however, these two perspectives—diagnose-fix and alleviate the symptom—carry the risk of a major pitfall: being transactional, they leave little room for exploration, consideration of alternatives, or listening for broader, systemic issues. Magda was known for her calm and empathic bedside manner, but she wasn't always as patient with colleagues or subordinates. It was a revelation to realize that to be an effective leader, she needed to focus on the big picture and create a space for dialogue. She also needed to listen with a deeper level of empathy and curiosity, and take time to reinforce what was working—celebrating and acknowledging success—to a greater degree than with her patients. Patients come and go, while colleagues are around for years. Becoming aware of your learned or hidden beliefs is not that difficult, but it requires self-reflection.

And just to be clear, I am not advocating that you alter your natural listening perspective in every situation. If you're sitting around the dinner table with a group of like-minded friends and everyone's viewpoint aligns with yours, then you're off to the races in terms of understanding one another. How satisfactory—and maybe a bit smug—it can feel when everyone gets to be right. But when we find ourselves in a situation with people with different or opposing values, opinions, and judgments, we can quickly run into a roadblock. (We see this every day on TV where panels of pundits volley back and forth in what is called "news." Unfortunately, this approach represents the very worst kind of listening.)

Here's the bottom line about listening perspectives: We all have them. We all bring to every conversation our training, cultural background, and values—none of which is inherently an obstacle to success. The goal for the flexible leader is to be on the lookout for ways to raise the periscope, widen the lens, and see through our stories.[2]

3. Choose Your Listening Persona

Research into what coach and psychologist Tatiana Bachkirova calls the "multiplicity of self" indicates that we all have multiple mini-selves. Think about the different ways you interact with colleagues, friends, family. The most effective coaches recognize that different circumstances require playing a variety of roles and can help their clients explore which ones feel restrictive and which might be liberating or expansive.[3]

Some training programs emphasize that a coach should play the role of a wise partner, asking broad, open-ended questions and supporting the client to find their own solutions; they tend to discourage offering advice or playing the role of mentor. Alternatively, if a coach has some specific expertise, such as a clinical psychology background or training in finance, they might find themselves playing the role of therapist if a client is feeling depressed, or consultant if a client is struggling with a financial dilemma. Most coach-training programs discourage taking on these roles, but a coaching dynamic—just like any human relationship—is fluid, and that ability to wear many hats may be just what their client needs.

One of the most common dilemmas I encounter with clients is when a peer—a colleague with whom they may have developed a friendship, or consider a confidant—is elevated into a leadership role, either as a direct boss or (common in today's flat organizations) as a project or matrixed manager. And the ones being promoted will ask, "Do I have to give up my friends? How do I garner respect as a leader from someone who just yesterday considered me a peer?"

I remind them, "Being a friend is a role. Being a leader is a role. Why can't you evolve your relationship to include a new role?" The key is to openly discuss the scope of the position with everyone impacted, acknowledge the different dynamic, and be transparent and thoughtful about boundaries.

Consider my CEO client who started a company with two friends, grew it to more than two thousand employees, and wound up having to fire one of his cofounders, while keeping the other not only as a trusted employee but as COO, a role that reports to him. The remaining cofounder carries a triple-whammy dynamic: He is an equal as cofounder; a direct report and subordinate to the CEO; and still a close friend. Both were early advocates of having a coach, and after a couple of productive years working together, they successfully added another role: They learned how to coach each other. If I were to ask Peter, the CEO, why this evolution worked so well with one of his cofounders but floundered with the third, Charles, his answer would be trite but true: Ego got in the way.

Charles could not "stomach" (as Peter put it) following his friend. He was so sensitive to slights and so insecure that he held on to the power of the title "cofounder"—all the way to the exit door. It was unfortunate, but I see it all the time. Peter was never able to dispel his friend's anxiety and feelings of diminishment at being subordinate. Charles chafed when Peter presented to the board, because he believed that he should be the one to do it. As the months went by and the conflict between them deepened, Charles's ego became more and more rigid, while Peter, learning from the experience how power dynamics can hurt relationships and curtail creativity, felt humbled and saddened by the loss.

To avoid any further ruptures, Peter learned how to switch roles while interacting with his other, happier cofounder and COO. They would sometimes go out for drinks but only to talk about families, newborns, vacations, and sports—not work. Work discussions were reserved for early morning coffee dates. These distinctions took discipline, and as they were working through an arrangement that ultimately felt satisfying to both, I had them reflect on how they maintained boundaries between work and home. Just like with Charles, being the founders of a start-up had wrecked a couple of relationships as they were entirely consumed with their jobs. And they came to see that a respectful marriage or personal relationship requires similar restraint: You need to know what role to play with your lover, your friends, your children. You can be it all but not all at once.

We are always playing a part, and we can learn to switch them as often as head surgeon Mark, my FIERCE role model, did the day I shadowed him. Yet too often we dive headlong into a meeting or conversation still wearing the hat from the last interaction. As Tatiana points out, effective leaders are aware of all the options available, and actively choose the one that is likely to be most useful in any given situation. In our personal lives, we are all familiar with this process. When one of our kids has a difficult day, or a friend calls for advice, we quickly become counselor or coach or confidant. But in the workplace, we seem to forget that we're chameleons. Being a leader means not becoming entrenched in habituated responses—*especially* the ones that got you promoted. Keep changing it up. Try out new ways of listening. And let your colleagues know. Don't keep it a secret or they may not notice or, worse, dismiss your changed behavior as fake!

Slow Down and Focus

Focus is a huge topic these days and we all know why: The rise of the smartphone has created an ADD culture. We are less able to focus in the moment because we are constantly being pinged by a wired world on text, email, and social media. Studies of the brain have shown how addictive this all can be. It is little wonder that every company wants to give you instant updates on every screen every hour of the day.

To make matters worse, somewhere along the way, the idea took root that multitasking is a good thing. It has become accepted in business culture that the more you can cram into a day, the better leader you will be. We all know on some level that this is bunk. But it is worse than we think. In the relentless drive for results, essential elements of flexible leadership get bypassed in the futile rush to complete our to-do lists. If you stop, breathe, and reflect, you will recognize immediately that multitasking is antithetical to listening. When people brag to you that they are great multitaskers—that they can text while driving, for example—be very wary. They are letting you know that they won't be able to pay attention for more than a few seconds, that an incoming text will be more important than anything you might say or do. Do you want to be this kind of leader? I doubt it.

While Magda did not have many of the unfocused multitasking habits that I've seen in other leaders, she could get caught up in missing-the-forest-for-the-trees syndrome, unaware of her impact on others, broader political or relationship dynamics, and the competing agendas of her colleagues, all because she was laser-focused on her goals. Although she was mindful within the scope of her projects, she was mindless elsewhere. I would go so far as to describe her approach not so much as multitasking but over-tasking—she plowed through her day with so many projects and such a long to-do list that she missed out on the bigger picture. On an emotional level, she sometimes failed to savor her achievements or celebrate the gifts of her team. She was never rude, and showed appreciation to her assistants and team members, but was often in a rush, which diminished the impact.

If you recognize yourself in Magda, don't despair. It is common for high-achieving leaders to get caught in a swirl of activity. To find a solution, we need to explore the differences between being focused (and awake) and busy (but asleep). There is a reason that meditation, focus, and mindfulness are finding wide purchase these days. Between our devices and responsibilities to friends, family, and work, it is no surprise that being focused and aware of the present moment is rare indeed. Yet no matter how busy we get, there is a tiny voice that pops through the noise occasionally with the truth that we all know: Life is happening *now*.

We all too often become stuck in mechanical ways of thinking and living. Have you ever sat down in front of the TV with a pint of ice cream, intent on enjoying a few spoonfuls and returning the rest to the freezer, only to look down twenty minutes later to find an empty container? This is a common example of mindlessness or being on autopilot. Some teachers talk about autopilot as a dreamlike state; we are not fully there. We fail to notice what our bodies are telling us.

Mindfulness is the opposite. It means switching off the cruise control and getting in the driver's seat of our attention again. Becoming mindful is simple, but antithetical to our Western mind-set. The scientific evidence is piling up about how much more effective—and healthier—we are when we practice being mindful, even for a minuscule amount of time.[4]

The good news is that it's well within your reach. Left to its own devices, your mind is typically a flood of thoughts without an anchor, but you can become mindful in just a few seconds. Try focusing on your breath, a soothing sound, or a physical object. Mindfulness is key to becoming self-aware, for it helps us quiet our internal chatter, even briefly, and become an observer of our own thoughts—an entry point for self-reflection. Jon Kabat Zinn, who famously developed the mindfulness program at Harvard that has brought the restorative and generative power of meditation into the mainstream, defines mindfulness as "Paying attention, on purpose, in the present moment, and non-judgmentally."

To get started with a mindfulness practice, schedule (yes, put them on your calendar!) small breaks, two or three moments a day, to breathe, walk in nature, or sit quietly. Commit to being consistent, because becoming mindful is a lifelong pursuit. Here are three suggestions to get you started.

1. Cerebral leaders: Use a meditation app such as Calm or Headspace and set aside ten minutes, twice a day, at specific times to sit quietly, breathe, and listen.

2. Emotional leaders: Same as above but add meditative or soothing music, which relieves anxiety and calms the heart.

3. Somatic leaders: Same as number 1 and number 2, but add a physical touchstone, such as a small rock or a piece of smooth beach glass, that you can hold in the palm of your hand to bring body awareness into your focus.

Get Curious

Curiosity may get a cat into trouble, but it is turning out to do just the opposite for humans. The latest research confirms that curiosity is a key attribute of highly successful leaders, which makes intuitive sense. Think about friends or colleagues you know who are naturally curious. They are not only interesting, but interested in a wide range of topics. They love to explore new ideas and are open to possibilities. Curious people are less likely to be resistant to change and may even foster it. They mix it up socially, being drawn to a variety of people and places. They are also more resilient when things go awry.[5]

But even the most curious among us are guilty of being selectively curious. At first blush, Magda was a curious type: She was not only interested in being coached but, unlike most clients, she also wanted to know and learn all about coaching! Yet feedback from her team indicated that she was more results focused than open-minded, that she had little patience for exploration or brainstorming. Magda was open to new ideas only if they had immediate application to improve workflow, or shored up the finances. But holding a dialogue for the sake of learning? Or trying out something that might fail or feel like a waste of time? Not so much.

How many times have you started down a path to learning something—wide-eyed and inquisitive—only to find yourself bored or frustrated when the subject matter got difficult or took you beyond your comfort zone? We have all been there! Curiosity may be crucial to your success as a leader, but it can be prone to confirmation bias: Just as most of us think we are good drivers (when the facts would indicate otherwise), most of us also consider ourselves curious— except when we're not.

For Magda, and for many of the physician leaders that I've coached over the years, the curiosity gene was in full bloom whenever the subject matter focused on the patient. Questions such as "How can we improve the process of patient care?" and "How can we see more people in a day yet maintain a high level of patient satisfaction?" sparked her curiosity. But questions about the team dynamic or how to better navigate the hospital bureaucracy would elicit a sigh, and had the opposite effect: They tended to shut her down.

The key to progress was simple, but not immediately obvious: Magda needed to broaden her listening perspective to recognize that the very thing she found boring was related to her primary interest, patient care. Topics such as cross-functional collaboration between her group (pain medicine) and other groups (pediatrics or surgery, for example) might have struck her as beside the point, but they were only one degree apart from patient care.

I told her that I had coached another physician who was struggling with a lack of patience and a reputation for being brusque who'd had a similar wake-up call. One of his bugaboos was the logistics group, which ensures that there are beds and linens and other crucial items in the inpatient rooms. He had so alienated the head of logistics and procurement with his frustration and impatience that one night his colleague casually flipped the switch on the circuit breaker that controlled all the lights in the hallways, leaving part of the hospital in total darkness. The nurses paged my client in a panic: We have no lights and can barely get to the patients! My client rushed to the hospital to discover the sabotage. When confronted the next day, the head of logistics demurred, "Oops." But his message was clear: Being dismissive with any aspect of hospital management would, in fact, impact the patients.

Magda found the story amusing, and a bit shocking, but she got the point. Curiosity is like a little candle of possibility that is always flickering within us, but can far too easily be extinguished with a few deep sighs and a stressed-out glance at our to-do list. I asked her to come to our next session with a short list of the topics she found most frustrating, those aspects of her job that seemed to stifle her creativity or shut her down.

"I don't need to wait until next week, Jeff," she replied immediately. "What frustrates me the most is my boss. I don't understand why he isn't more supportive. Why is he always getting in the way of my projects and cutting me off at the knees when I want to move ahead with a new initiative?" I suggested Magda take on her *boss,* Tim, as a project. If he was not supportive, but they had the same goals—great patient care, a financially sustainable practice, innovation in service delivery—what could be causing this disconnect?

Where she lacked an understanding of his behavior, she had not bothered to try to get an explanation, and she had to admit that on some level she was curious about his motives. This required Magda to extend herself to her boss in a way that was initially uncomfortable: She asked him to meet for lunch "just to discuss how we work together." I wish I had been a fly on the wall! It went so great that she suggested they meet more often for personal check-ins and told him she would value his mentorship. Of course, that was exactly what he had been waiting to hear, but since his style was similarly action oriented, assertive, and rarely personal or vulnerable, he had also failed to reach out.

For Magda, that was just the tip of the iceberg. She came to see other spots where her natural curiosity was underleveraged: working with nurses, exploring process and patient improvements, seeking outside vantage points, and networking and building relationships with people outside her normal day-to-day.

Studies have found that innovative organizations exhibit core attributes that every leader, whether alpha or beta, should keep in mind:

1. They support risk-taking (within limits) and don't punish failures. If employees fear being punished for ideas that don't work or failed attempts at trying something new, they will quickly get the message "Don't rock the boat."

2. They provide space and support for reflection and creativity time.

3. They empower people by pushing ownership and accountability across and down.

4. They encourage associates to get out of the bubble and engage in activities with competitors, other industries, other cultures, and so forth. Outside perspectives are often what are needed to bring the best ideas in-house; not every idea can be homegrown.

From Beta to Alpha

A walk on the beach at sunset was an auspicious and memorable way to kick off a coaching engagement. And that is exactly where Renaldo first brought up the possibility of working with me. After a long, rather grueling day of workshops with him and his managers, everyone needed a break. Since our off-site session was being held at a beautiful resort on the far eastern shore of North Carolina, the fact that it was still early spring, and rather windy and chilly, didn't prevent the group from spilling onto the beach as soon as I let them loose. What was unusual was when Renaldo pulled me aside and asked me to walk with him along the shore. As the sun slowly sank behind us and we strolled ankle-deep in the cool waters of the Atlantic, Renaldo shared that his boss, the chief marketing officer, had suggested that he join the coaching program I had been conducting for other senior leaders at their e-commerce retail start-up. I remember thinking that rarely had someone approached me with such a self-deprecating, almost sheepish tone.

"To be honest, I'm not really sure how coaching could help me," he said. "Josh seems to think that I'm too nice. He told me that I need to get tougher with my people, be more forceful in holding them accountable. I'm not sure that I want to do that if it means becoming more dictatorial like him. I feel good about the way my team interacts. I respect the opinions of my folks. I learn a lot from them when we have brainstorming sessions. But I have heard the scuttlebutt, too. Some people think that my meetings are too open-ended and take up too much time. I guess the talk got back to Josh, and he thinks I need to be more directive. I wonder, is there a middle ground?"

"I get it," I replied. "It can be a curse for a leader to be open and a good listener. It's downright ironic to be asked to coach someone to become, well, bossier. I observed your group interactions today, and noticed that you raised the most questions that prompted people to share. You were great at collecting input from everyone around the table. I'd love to see more of my clients be able to do that well."

And with that, I embarked on a coaching engagement with another young leader who contradicts most of the stereotypes.

A true beta leader, Renaldo's great strength as a manager of data science in a high-tech environment is that he treats his subordinates as equals. I was impressed with his ability to conduct a brainstorming session that was both inclusive and generative. At the same time, in the context of what I've mentioned before—every strength can become a liability—I noticed that Renaldo was challenged with driving to a result. While some of the other small groups that I worked with that day were competitive and focused on coming up with the answer, Renaldo's team meandered from topic to topic, continuing to work long past the time when everyone else was taking a coffee break. I could see that his beta style of leadership had already become a barrier to success.

The core question with a beta is clear: How does a leader with a consensus-oriented, inquisitive nature become more results oriented and decisive? Renaldo was not an introvert looking to become more expressive or confident. In fact, the reason Renaldo was promoted to manage the data science team, an essential function where marketing analytics are key drivers of success, is that he had a strong background in the space. He could be forceful and take charge. His natural tendency, however, was not so much to drive for an answer as to continuously explore alternatives.

This showed up acutely when Renaldo was asked to deliver a presentation describing the results of his team's work. Given fifteen minutes to summarize quarterly results and make recommendations, Renaldo showed up with a forty-page deck and a long list of how further analytics studies could support the business. It was all great stuff but way too much, way too long, and way too detailed. It saddened me to look around the room and witness his colleagues' eye rolls.

"We have work to do," I explained. "You don't have to become bossy or autocratic, but you do need to get in touch with your inner competitor. You do need to step up and learn to be assertive at the appropriate times. The good news is that it is not an either-or proposition: You can do both."

If you can relate to Renaldo, then you may be one of those leaders who is ahead of the game in the current business paradigm. Millennials who work for you most likely appreciate your willingness to listen, your desire to make decisions based on consensus, and your openness to explore rather than always push for results. Trouble is, these strengths can backfire when your superiors or peers are more like Magda—pushing to get things done, fast. Your challenge is to recognize the value of being assertive when the situation calls for it while still committing to continuous learning. In this case, learn to flex.

Quick-Hit Workout: Alpha to Beta

LISTENING PRESENCE

1. **Speak less, listen more:** Ask a buddy to monitor your volume when it comes to speaking versus listening. You don't need to tell them a percentage to shoot for, just that you are trying to improve your listening skills. There is no right or wrong amount. If you're naturally an alpha, your goal is to speak a bit less, listen a bit more.

2. **Get comfortable with silence:** Choose a touchstone that will provide a reminder to be okay with short silences in group discussions and one-on-one meetings. Some clients choose to sit on their hands (it shifts your energy and makes you pay attention); write "Quiet is okay" on the top of a notepad and place it in front of them; or hold an actual stone that sends a signal to their brain to be quiet and listen (I use a small, beach-weathered heart-shaped stone that fits in the palm of my hand).

3. **Plan open-ended questions in advance:** Find starter questions that build on each other: "How?" "What?" "Why?" and the like. Add to your list the compounding statement "Tell me more." (You might post this on your computer, phone, or notepad as a

reminder.) Practice opening statements that invite people to share, such as "I'm curious" and "I would love to hear ..."

LISTENING PERSPECTIVE

4. **Know your agenda so you can drop your agenda:** Beyond the topics that you likely put together for each meeting, write down in advance what you hope to accomplish or plan together. The more you can become aware of your intentions, the more likely they won't trip you up when it is time to let it go.

5. **Listening tour:** Whenever possible, see if you can drop your agenda and instead explore the goals of others. Consider yourself on an expedition to learn instead of having a destination to reach.

LISTENING PERSONA

6. **Clarify your role:** Take time to reflect on the most effective role you could take that would support your goal in your interaction with others. Consider whether you want to be a coach, a teacher, a partner, a friend, an investigator, or someone else.

7. **Switch hats:** Look for a role model who plays a variety of roles in their leadership capacity, especially one who behaves differently from the way you would tend to. Put on your investigator hat and analyze what they do that works—then try out new ways of speaking and listening, by following their lead.

SLOW DOWN AND FOCUS

8. **Mindful minute:** Set a timer for one minute, then put it aside. Sit up straight, in a quiet location where you will not be disturbed. Take three deep breaths—and focus your attention on breathing. Observe what it feels like to switch from an inhale to

an exhale. Close your eyes and feel your body as it circulates the breath. Notice your thoughts: Do they stay focused or drift away? If the latter, that's okay. Just gently bring your attention back to your nostrils and the air flowing in and out.

9. **Buffer zones:** Schedule five-minute breaks between meetings. During these buffer zones, find some physical movement to engage your body; walking or getting outdoors can bring a huge shift in your mental state. Just five minutes away from our desks engages those emotional, somatic, or mental aspects we tend to neglect, and the results can be almost miraculous—depending on what we need, waking us up or quieting us down to move into our next activity with greater self-awareness and equanimity.

10. **"Me" time:** I have all my clients block out certain times each week for reflection. This may feel selfish, or if you are always in demand, impossible, yet even the top CEOs in the world optimize their mental and physical energy by committing to "me" time, and making it sacred. Start with just an hour a week. With regularity and commitment to this practice, you will become more productive, creative, and relaxed, even when life seems crazy.

GET CURIOUS

11. **Engage your beginner's mind:** What does "play" mean to you? Playing a sport or a musical instrument, or writing or painting? Make time to learn a new skill, one that is both enjoyable and strenuous enough to stretch your mind. One of my clients adds her own version of playtime to her business trips around the world: short stints exploring a new neighborhood, window-shopping, or visiting a museum.

12. **Monday Morning Mavericks:** Hold regular meetings for exploration with your team. One of my clients starts each week with Monday Morning Mavericks, a meeting where he encourages everyone to bring an idea inspired by what they did over the weekend.

Quick-Hit Workout: Beta to Alpha

1. **Unleash your inner competitor:** Revisit a time when you had to compete to win or achieve a goal. What did you do to focus? What was your winning formula? Reconnect to this energy and make a list of the activities that you did to get there.

2. **Three's the limit:** Limit your meeting agendas to three items or less. If you can get it down to just one item, all the better. Especially if you have a reputation for lengthy, overly free-flowing sessions, people will appreciate your shift to a "quick-hit" style. You can still leave time for feedback and dialogue, but with fewer items to digest, you will be more focused and able to optimize discussions.

3. **Short is sweet:** Manage the length of your written communications—email, PowerPoint, and the like. Review the length, quality, and tone of colleagues who you think are excellent communicators, then give yourself a rule to follow what they do, such as "two paragraphs" or "three bullets."

4. **The declaration:** Journal about your strengths. It is important for beta leaders in particular to be clear about what they are good at—and to take a stand for it, as appropriate. Take the VIA Survey (a free strengths and values assessment that you can find

at viacharacter.org), then write your top one or two strengths as an "I am . . ." declaration. Practice stating them out loud to yourself, to confidants, and to anyone who can coach you to bring more confidence into your daily work.

Assuming you have tapped into your growth mind-set for this chapter, are you clear yet on what you need to do to flex your leadership style? No matter how flexible you feel today, growing means reflecting on how you listen, how you focus, how you make decisions, and how you incorporate new ideas. Are you curious? Can you be directive and assertive when necessary? The ideal leader is neither all alpha or all beta, but either (or both!) as the context requires.

If you are somatically inclined, think about developing flexibility like a workout for mental agility: No matter where you fall on the spectrum, you can build and tone the muscle of flexibility by becoming aware of the story you tell yourself about your leadership style and seeking to build on whatever works.

CHAPTER 4

Be Intentional: From Einstein's Space to Van Gogh's Sky

The book you hold in your hands is a vehicle for communication. If you have come this far and not set it aside, if the words on the page still hold your attention, then on some visceral level, we have connected, you and me. We are communicating. When you cuddle up on the sofa with a good novel and find yourself entranced, losing track of time, drawn into a world of the artist's creation, you are in what I would call "deep dialogue" with the writer. But what is it about a compelling novel, or a useful self-help book, that keeps that dialogue alive? Why is it that some leaders can hold their team in rapt attention with their vision, their ambitious goals, their call for action, while others fall flat, leaving subordinates disengaged, or worse?

As a coach, I have seen highly talented leaders stumble in their quest to create impact and build followers because they failed to reflect on how they *communicate* their message. As we move into the subject of intentional communication—how you reach across the physical, emotional, and intellectual spaces that divide people—ask yourself, "How is this book connecting with me?" Are you resonating with case studies that speak directly to your experience? Are you skimming the suggested practices, or taking note of the ones that make sense or feel practical for you?

Of course, as an author, my fantasy is that you will read and relish every word I write. But who am I kidding? That is not how I read self-help books, so why would it be any different for you? We all have our own affinities for what information impacts us deeply and what we tend to dismiss. As psychologist Lawrence LeShan and physicist Henry Margenau write in *Einstein's Space and Van Gogh's Sky*:

> The possibilities open to artists [and, I would add, leaders] are also limited by the cultural viewpoint within which they live. Each culture makes certain approaches to the infinite possible. It makes other approaches impossible or incomprehensible. A cartoon published several years ago showed a studio of a Renaissance painter sitting next to typical paintings of the period. In a corner was the famed Mondrian painting of 1921, *Composition with Red Yellow and Blue*. The painter was explaining it to a friend, "Oh, that's just something I tried which didn't work out." Of those attempts at the organization of reality made by its artists [and scientists], each culture selects some as successful and rejects others. What the culture selects then helps shape that culture.

Our culture has come to toggle between fact and fiction with great agility—such that we are deeply susceptible to losing the threads of truth and meaning. A connective tissue of communication between leader and follower needs to include a balance of evidence and anecdote, shared with humility. There is no one right way to communicate. I choose to share both stories and evidence for what seems to work. But every situation and every individual is unique. Your goal is to become aware of your gifts as a communicator, learn from others, and raise the bar by expanding your view of reality to include both Einstein's space—the science, the facts, the evidence that bolsters a position—and the story and beauty of Van Gogh's sky. Each is important. Each brings us together.

Today, we seem to have a great deal of trouble even determining what facts are, with the headlines full of "fake news" and conspiracy theories considered by a significant minority of the population to be real. Likewise, you've probably heard the phrase "evidence-based" all over the place, as if we have finally conquered the conundrum of empiricism: how to bolster a theory with evidence, such that it can be verified and held as a gold standard. Yet this is rarely the case.

Neuroscientists are the first ones to exercise caution when they hear about studies of the brain being promulgated in popular media to "prove" why we do the things we do. Some coaches use functional magnetic resonance imaging (fMRI) studies of physical changes in the brain to declare that they understand how best to motivate people, or how to coach them. Of course, I include some fascinating neuroscience studies in this book, which can be helpful in understanding the chemical and neuronal processes that occur when we process data, integrate signals from the body, respond to stimuli, and make decisions. But to conclude that we now understand the essence of what were previously mysteries—memory, consciousness, emotions, the connection between our inner and outer worlds—or that we can elevate human performance purely through "brain-based coaching," would be a stretch.

As I said, the scientists themselves remain their own greatest skeptics—for the more we learn about the brain, the more that remains unknown. It's paradoxical: We are using the very tool we don't fully understand to uncover how the tool works. It is important to keep this in mind (no pun intended), or we risk coming to believe that we are not so different from machines. So it is with a grain of salt that we follow the path of "evidence." Good science is important because it clears up confusion and moves us toward deeper knowledge of how to be most effective, but it doesn't replace the story, the vision, or the mystery of imagination, which is what inspires leaders to lead and the rest of us to follow.[1]

End with the Beginning in Mind

No matter how successful we became, I never forgot the struggles, the dreams, and the commitment of our tiny team in those early days. People ask me whether I think we were lucky—just sort of found ourselves with the right tech product at the right time. I always scoff at that. The truth is that our success was hardly preordained. It was the wild, wild West in the software world—and here we were way out in the middle of nowhere [on the outskirts of Paris]. From the very beginning, when it was just me and Bernard, on to the next three hires, and on and on until we had over a thousand employees, I would share my dream of changing the way people make decisions using technology, and I always felt the love—and that is the right word, love—that the team had for what we were doing. So, in a sense, I always knew that we would be a success. No matter how many starts and stalls and ups and downs we had, my job was to keep the passion, the initial spark that stoked our fire, alive. Makes me proud and

humble—but very clear: Success at the end is always about
the heart at the beginning.

These profound words came from Denis Payre, sitting across the
table from me in a diner in Boston that suited this super-successful
leader just fine, as it represented his core style—down-to-earth—and
preference for connection—face-to-face. Being with Denis, almost
twenty years after he was one of my first coaching clients, I was trans-
ported back to the halcyon days of the dot-com era, when the first
signs emerged of how impactful the Internet and its tools would
become.

I want to share Denis's story not because of the amazing achievements of his firm, Business Objects, which was ultimately sold for
many millions. No, I want to share the lesser-known story about *why*
they were so prosperous—and how you can learn, as I did, what it
takes to fuel the growth of a company from start-up to scale-up to
success beyond your wildest dreams. Of course, it takes a great
product and good timing, but it takes something else as well: great
leadership and powerful, inspiring communication. In Bernard and
Denis, Business Objects had all of the above and more.

Le Start-Up

The nineties were a heady time. Dot-coms were springing up like
mushrooms. The Internet was ascendant, as were software entrepreneurs. For young engineers with a knack for coding and a taste for
risk, the future seemed bright. It was a time not unlike today, but a
bit wilder. Enter Denis Payre and Bernard Liautaud. These two smart,
intense young French guys, one a marketing genius, the other an
analytical engineer, quietly changed the world of business

decision-making forever. Today, Business Objects is part of the software empire of German conglomerate SAP, with more than eighty-five thousand employees.

In the early days, Denis and Bernard shared an office. They were great friends and complementary partners. Both were strong alpha leaders, coming across as tough, analytical, and forceful. Yet all it took was witnessing one town-hall gathering of all the employees—of which there were perhaps fifty at the time, mostly engineers and a few salespeople—to see that their communication styles could not have been more different. Bernard was the numbers guy. Powered up with slides of forecasts and budgets, he would wade through the details of product design, all logic, data, and strategy. As an engineer and an introvert, he could be confident and decisive, but his affect was flat, businesslike. Over the years that I worked with him and coached him, he expanded his storytelling repertoire and learned to communicate with more passion, but he would always be the quiet one, reserved and a bit uncomfortable on a stage.

Denis was an alpha leader, but entirely beta in front of an audience. A salesperson by training, he had developed a powerful ability to read the room. He knew how to connect with a group, not by delivering data or reading bullets from a slide, but by orchestrating a dialogue, his prepared remarks coming across as spontaneous, even off the cuff (although they weren't). He was inspirational, because he always began with an anecdote about his personal goals for the company, and ended with a call to action: "My friends, it is time for France to have its own Silicon Valley . . . and together we can make that dream come true." Is it any wonder that Denis became a politician soon after selling his stake in Business Objects ten years later?

With presence and passion, Denis connected the dots for his staff, reminding them every time he took to the stage that Business Objects was not just a software company. It was a special club made up of France's best and brightest, who would give Silicon Valley a run for their money.

Why Communication Matters

What Denis knew intuitively, anyone can learn: The essence of communication is emotional connection. Whether it's a tweet or a text or email, it is the *feeling* that people glom on to. Strong communication can push people to act—sometimes even against their best interests. In recent years, we have learned just how certain linguistic patterns influence the network connections between the amygdala (the brain's seat of emotions) and the prefrontal cortex (the rational decision maker).

When Russell Gonnering and Julie Lein at Arizona State University studied how the brain reacts to certain political speeches, advertisements, and what they call "performance poetry," it turned out that memorable phrases, a high pitch, monosyllabic words, and songlike patterns (for example, alliteration and rhymes) influence the brain's limbic system to move information more quickly through to the prefrontal cortex. In other words, we are not only enamored by sweet talk itself, we are also intoxicated by the *sounds* of our most effective orators. These sorts of studies provide evidence to support what most coaches have always known: how a leader shows up, how she communicates, and her intention, tone, and inflection, matter.

The Neuroscience of Communication

Using a more narrative approach is not at all mutually exclusive with reporting facts or setting goals. But for today's workers to be motivated by those goals, they must feel a personal connection to the purpose behind a new initiative or business. Intentional communication is not either-or. Great communicators still lay out plans and project the possibilities for sales, revenue growth, customer retention, and the like. What they add to the mix, however, is the *why*: why it matters to them, and why it should matter to others, from passion and vision to broader context and meaning—to goals and plans—and back to the core raison d'être. Including a personal story is the first step toward shifting strategic communication toward aspirational communication. The second step is connecting to the audience on an emotional level.

In just a few years, neuroscience has come a long way in understanding how the brain processes emotion, but much of it is still a mystery; the reasons why we have emotions in the first place, and why we are aware of them beyond a survival instinct, remain elusive. What we know is that the amygdala, the seat of emotion, is located behind the prefrontal cortex (where rational thoughts are processed) and in front of the basal ganglia, or reptilian brain, which is responsible for our core instincts. Studies of brain scans and hormonal levels (cortisol, dopamine, and oxytocin, in particular) show that the brain is activated by strong emotions, both positive and negative, and those emotions are influenced by a multitude of signals. As we discussed in the last chapter, the emotional transmittal process is complex and involves all five senses: words, tone, proximity, facial and body expressions, and physical presence of a speaker.

When we think about effective communication, how to connect with others becomes a crucial question. Keep in mind that as infants our ability to communicate with our caregivers started long before we learned to speak. The amygdala develops that sense of connection, either with positive feelings, such as safety, belonging, and love, or negative feelings, including insecurity, disconnection, and aloneness, through what are called mirror neurons. This network of cells in the amygdala is engaged in response to facial expressions, touch, tone, and other stimuli. Words come later. Even as adults sitting in a conference room, we respond with emotional resonance or dissonance even before our boss opens his mouth to tell us about the latest strategic plan. Do we trust this person? Feel safe? This kind of feedback is always at work beneath the surface, and drives how we feel about the speaker.

If you think about the developmental process in infants, you won't be surprised to learn that storytelling carries a greater emotional resonance than facts and figures. Whether we are talking about the neurological development of the brain or the story of our origins as a species, the fact is that humans have been coming together to share stories for millennia. Ultimately, business organizations are tribal configurations holed up in office buildings or connected through virtual networks, based around a shared sense of belonging—the glue of which is a story.

Core to the culture of any successful firm is its origin story, which may start out as "a couple of guys in a garage" but over time takes on a mythic power, as it gets repeated over and over, gaining clarity and color and detail. Denis understood this, and harkened back to the beginning at every step along the way. The story takes on a life of its own. Inspiring people to act in alignment with a vision is always connected to a common history, cause, or movement, whether overt or assumed. It is simply in our DNA.

Alpha to Beta and Back

It's really tough to know if we're good communicators. You may receive feedback from a boss, peer, or subordinate, which can be helpful, but it is important to probe more deeply, especially if the feedback is generic, for example, "Nancy's communication skills are fine, very professional and clear." This is a start but doesn't even begin to get to the heart of your unique strengths or opportunities for expansion. If you want to grow as a communicator, you need to know how your presence, tone, and pace are received by others.

Here's where a feedforward exercise can help. Instead of asking for feedback from your employees or boss, seek out a colleague whom you trust and ask them to share one thing that you could do better when communicating in a professional setting. Don't ask if they think you are "good" or "bad"—just to focus on how you could improve.

Another great option is to think about someone who is particularly adept at telling personal stories, connecting with an audience, and inspiring action from others. Think about what they do at a granular level: What words do they use? Stories? Humor? Jokes? What are the specifics of their body language? What is their tone? Pace? What gestures and facial expressions do they use?

Get even more detailed: How do they position their body? Do they stand still or move? What do they do with their hands? What about eye contact? How, where, and when do they look at the audience? What is the level of intensity of their gaze? If you were to give them advice on how to improve, what would you say? How do they begin and end their talks? Why do you think they are so powerful? What could you do to emulate them?

The deeper you can reflect about the way someone communicates well, the more you can learn. I remember catching Denis rehearsing just before giving an important update to his staff. In the heat of the actual presentation, he would go off script and riff about a client or a past victory, but it was because he had rehearsed the core of his message many, many times that he was comfortable and calm enough to appear spontaneous.

If you took the time to get feedback on the Leadership Agility Self-Assessment at the beginning of this book, then you know whether you are perceived as more alpha (data driven, fact based, analytical), or beta (narrative, emotive, purpose driven) in your style. If you came out stronger on the alpha side, don't despair! These are important skills for a communicator as well. As I said, it is not an either-or proposition. Remember, Denis's gift was his ability to switch between alpha and beta. He was not always waxing poetic, but he knew how to do it and when. If you are more of an analytical communicator, start to think about how you can pump up your emotional connection with images and metaphors.

Let's take a closer look at how one highly successful leader enhanced her communication style with beta qualities. Then we'll skip to the other end of the spectrum and consider that rare breed: a top-notch beta communicator who goes overboard. See if you recognize yourself in either example. Reflect on the coaching they received and consider what worked to help them increase their impact. With this in mind, you can coach yourself!

The Awkward Alpha

No one would consider Suzanne a wallflower. Confident and assertive, she is the five-foot-five-inch powerhouse leader of the intensive care unit at a prestigious academic hospital in the Midwest, with dozens of primary care doctors, anesthesiologists, and intensivists in her charge. She's accomplished what few women in medicine have, reaching the level of department head (only 14 percent of hospital top execs are female). With multiple awards for research and patient care, Suzanne is a superb scientist and a renowned physician. I worked closely with her on the implementation of a leadership training and coaching program for her team leaders, all of whom respected and followed her willingly—and generally liked her as a person, even if they didn't always appreciate her brusque style.

So it was a bit of a shock to me when I attended a faculty meeting about six months in to observe her in action and found myself in a half-empty room. Where was everyone? I knew that there were more than sixty physicians and at least that many nurses and technicians in the department. I also knew that their monthly meetings were one of the only times when Suzanne would update the entire department on issues that directly impacted their lives: compensation, benefits, work hours, new recruits, and the financial status of the division. These meetings were not something to be taken lightly—and she was even providing dinner and wine! And yet, where were they?

The cause became clear as soon as she took the floor and began a monotone recitation of her bullet points. When Suzanne finished her presentation and opened the floor for questions, more than three-quarters of the seats were empty. She did a great job of appearing upbeat and engaging with the few questions from the folks that were left, but her unease in speaking to a nearly deserted room wasn't lost on me.

Suzanne herself was painfully aware of the lack of engagement in her meetings. When I brought it up to her in a follow-up session, she acknowledged that public speaking was her Achilles' heel. She hated it. Having been trained at the world's top universities, she knew what an engaging presentation looked like, but she struggled with stage fright and anxiety, even in front of her own people, and fell victim to what we in the trade call "DPP: Death by PowerPoint." Like many of us who find presenting nerve-racking, she had long since given up on improving her performance, and instead focused on what she knew best: data. She told herself that her goal was to transmit information, and at that she was a success. Of course, success is relative, and having more than half the department either not show or quietly slip out the back hardly qualified. When I gently confronted her, she agreed. "But what can I do? Presenting is just not my thing. I'm a scientist, not a performer. My people need to accept me for who I am."

"All true," I agreed, "but you are so personable one-on-one. There is no reason why you can't be more personable with a group."

From that moment we were off exploring the narrative arc that made Suzanne tick. I asked her to share a story or two about how and why she had chosen to become an intensivist. She moved me to tears with anecdotes about helping a family come together at the bedside of a dying matriarch, arranging for them to sneak in some incense, a candle, and music so that they could all connect with a beautiful ritual during the patient's final hours. Suzanne had realized early in her medical training that dealing with the very sick, while excruciatingly hard work, was also immensely gratifying.

As I listened to her describe the deep heart connection she had with her patients, and her excitement about studying intensive care procedures and ethics—all with the intention of making a patient's most painful and perhaps final moments as bearable as possible—the true humanity of this remarkable human being came to the surface. I said to her, "It struck me at the meeting that you were all business, but you are clearly much more than that. Why don't you share a story or two about your work with patients with the team?"

"Ah." She sighed. "Doctors can be a cynical bunch, Jeff. They've heard it all before—or maybe even been there themselves. I'm not sure they want to hear me wax poetic." She had a point. But I wasn't convinced. Doctors may have seen it all, but it seemed to me that they would be inspired to hear that their boss was not just in her office running numbers, but down and dirty where it mattered—with patients. At one point, she reached into her desk and pulled out a photo of a group of people all cuddled up on a patient's bed. "This family was so amazing," she said. "The patient died quietly only a few moments after I took this. . . ." She trailed off.

I suggested that Suzanne make two simple changes when presenting: 1. Open with a story about why she continues to love her work, and share a visual, like a photo, of a patient, maybe someone who recovered or whose family she supported during a difficult time; and 2. End by reconnecting to the opening picture, and ask someone on her team to share their own story in answer to the question "Why do we do what we do?" Begin with a story. End with a story. But not just any story—one that connects you to the work, something that you deeply care about, something that feels vulnerable to share. I promised her that people would suffer through the facts and figures if they felt more of a connection. All she had to do was bring more of herself to the stage—flesh and blood, head and heart.

By now you have guessed the ending of this story. It worked. The engagement levels at her meetings skyrocketed—and the irony is that the basic messaging hadn't changed that much (although I did recommend focusing on the audience and not on her bullets as much as possible).

If you can relate to any aspect of Suzanne's journey, here are the simple action steps:

1. Open with a story that reconnects you (and your audience) to the reason you do what you do. Suzanne always brought the group in to share their stories as well, so that it wasn't just about her.

2. Use props—a video, photo, music—to enhance the story, like a letter of gratitude that a patient had written about one of Suzanne's people.

3. End with another story, maybe a story of possibility, like a vision for the future. Suzanne shared her dream of a more family-oriented intensive care unit, down to the aesthetics, the support infrastructure, and architecture and design.

Buttoning Up a Beta

Is it possible to have too much of a good thing? What if you communicate *too* much? Share too many moving stories? Display too much emotion?

Occasionally I have been called in to coach a leader who is so beta on the leadership assessment that he acquires a reputation for being "off the cuff" or "glib"—as was the case with Brendan, a project leader whose boss wanted him to have more, as she put it, "gravitas." Brendan had recently fumbled a presentation about a product rollout to a group of senior executives.

Standing on the precipice of becoming a senior VP at a global pharmaceutical firm, Brendan was assessed by his colleagues and superiors in a classic 360-feedback initiative as a great manager—a good coach and motivating communicator—but as overly jocular at times, and a bit too extemporaneous, leading the C-suite executives to worry that he wasn't always up to speed, or that under pressure he might not be totally trustworthy. The feedback was telling: "Brendan is an outstanding manager, who clearly knows his product and people, but he tends to go 'off-script' too much, responding to serious questions from colleagues with funny anecdotes and long-winded stories—all of which are quite entertaining, but beside the point. Brendan needs to know when to 'button up' and stick with the facts."

A first-rate executive in many ways, Brendan was extroverted, friendly, affable, open, and, as you might imagine, a consummate storyteller. Growing up in a working-class neighborhood in a country town in Scotland, he'd had to fend for himself and channeled his energy into rugby. He learned early on how to deflect anger and danger—especially when facing down his father—with a funny story. It was a skill that would hold him in good stead all the way up the corporate ladder—until it started to backfire.

Brendan was fully aware of how his style and his tendency to try to entertain sometimes got him into trouble. It was the storyteller in him that fired his emotions, which in turn energized others. But he recognized the limitations of humor and spontaneity, especially when a multimillion-dollar product launch was on the line. Throughout our time together, he was intent on examining and changing his pattern of, as he put it, "winging it."

"It's ironic; my problem is that I love giving presentations," he said. "I love speaking to my team and getting us all energized with a vision of what we can accomplish. I'm more bored by the day-to-day stuff—so when I can bring the team together and share stories about our accomplishments, or dig in together to work through the challenges, that's when it gets fun for me. Maybe I should have been a stand-up comic instead of a drug developer!"

Motivated to coach himself, he came up with a game plan. Before the next presentation with senior management, he committed to doing the following: 1. Simplify the message: Focus on a few key points to disseminate the information his audience needed to hear. Share one personal story, but only if that story illuminated his takeaways. 2. Stick close to the facts: Follow the lead of his colleagues, whose backgrounds in science had led them to respect the data. 3. Hack the humor: Brendan would never be a stoic, bullet-driven presenter, but he came to see that his jokes were best doled out sparingly so as not to undermine his credibility.

By the end of our engagement, he said, "It's in my nature to lighten things up. Scientists and finance types tend to take themselves so seriously. But I understand now that humor must add, not subtract, from my presence as a leader. On the other hand, Jeff, I've got to be me: I'll always want to leave them laughing." At this, of course, we chuckled together.

Quick-Hit Workout: Alpha to Beta

1. **Make it personal:** *What is your why?* Take time to explain how the presentation connects with your story, your vision, your dreams. If you're not sure, grab a notebook and review your life in five-year increments, writing down the high and low moments of each period. Ask yourself, "How did these crucial moments impact who I am today?"

2. **Know your audience:** *What is their why?* Reflect on who your audience is and what they most want to learn from you. What is their goal in attending your presentation? Why do they care about your work? How can you inspire them to act?

3. **Paint a picture:** *Make it visual.* Whenever possible, use imagery: either actual visuals—a picture, cartoon, or diagram—or a story built around a parable, poem, or song.

Quick-Hit Workout: Beta to Alpha

1. **Pin the point:** *Start with the end in mind.* What are the fundamental takeaways for your audience? Dialogue and storytelling are great ways to connect, but limit yourself to a maximum of five key points, no matter how many memorable anecdotes you share to get there.

2. **Button up:** *Stick with the script.* If you tend to digress, slip into brainstorm mode, or think out loud, write down your key points and memorize them. You may want to enlist a buddy in the audience to sit in the front row and act as your timekeeper to make sure you stay on track.

3. **One story, multiple messages:** *Pick the best story.* The adage holds: Less is more. One personal story that connects a key takeaway to your vision—your "why"—is best.

4. **Hack the humor:** *Focus your funny bone.* Take stock of how you typically use humor: Do you tell humorous anecdotes? Jokes? Are you sarcastic? These can all be effective, or they can be a distraction. Use feedforward to get input from someone you trust about which might be most powerful for your purposes.

PART II

Emotional Leadership

CHAPTER 5

The Elephant in the Room Runs the Show

"If you could just get Rachel to be a bit less emotional, I'd be thrilled. As you could see in the meeting with her and Michael, she just comes across as so intense. It's great that she's such a passionate advocate for her people, but she puts everyone on the defensive because her arguments are unfiltered and dramatic." Joseph was the senior leader of an engineering team who was trying to get two of his project managers to "play nice" and share resources. I can't tell you how many times I've heard a similar request from a male executive: Just get her (it is almost always *her*) to be less emotional, and all will be well.

Every leader needs to be aware of their feelings, know how and when to express emotion, and be sensitive to how their reactions impact others, of course. But here's the rub: In that very same session, in which Joseph was hoping that I would get Michael and Rachel to collaborate, here's what I observed: *Michael* was the emotional one. He was forceful, assertive, unfiltered, and downright pushy in his desire to get his way and protect "his people." To top it off, when it was clear that the final so-called compromise had come down in his favor, he got up from the table, crossed the room, and gave a very nonplussed Rachel a bear hug. She rolled her eyes for my benefit, but didn't say anything. For hours, I kept thinking about that moment. Raising the possibility that hugging a female colleague during a meeting bordered on harassment might have put both Michael and Joseph on the defensive, but I'm sure there would have been less hugging going on if there were only men in the room.

Joseph respected both of his leaders but clearly had a soft spot for Michael, and didn't seem to notice his emotionality (or the hug). Rachel, on the other hand, who was passionate but calm, got pegged as overly demonstrative. Sad to say, this lopsided drama plays out in conference rooms across the country. The double standard and unconscious bias that says women are "emotional" where men are "assertive" is alive and well and, if anything, *increasing* in intensity as women expand their leadership roles.

You don't have to take my word for it: A recent survey found that more than six hundred executives perceived women to be less effective in competencies such as "strategic planning," "decision-making," and "delegating," because they exhibited a "feminine" (read: emotional) style.[1] And 50 percent of those surveyed were women! Women, in fact, are all too often the harshest judges of their counterparts. (Respondents did not exclusively admonish women; men, too, who were deemed more "feminine" in their leadership style were considered less effective.) The good news is that diversity programs and leadership development initiatives are now placing more emphasis on raising our awareness of gender-based bias and harassment in the workplace. Sexual harassment scandals involving celebrities and political leaders have cast a bright light on unethical behavior that has gone on for decades, if not centuries. Change is afoot—and it's long overdue.

Why does this matter? Simply put, because we are all emotional beings. Whenever there is a conflict, emotions are the elephant in the room. How we perceive the value and impact of those responses colors how we view our colleagues. Even in the midst of an evolution toward post-heroic leadership, where emotional intelligence is not only recognized but considered *crucial* to effectiveness, emotions are still persona non grata in many executive suites. I encourage my female clients (and men with a predisposition toward emotionally driven leadership) to become keenly aware of the bias they may face, and to develop strategies for managing the perceptions of others. This does not mean you should hide feelings, but rather pay attention to how you express them in different contexts. When the elephant of emotion is running the show, the trick is to do three things: 1. Recognize your feelings; 2. Manage how you express them, both verbally and nonverbally; and 3. Be sensitive to how they are perceived by others. The next two chapters focus on how to do all three.

But before we jump into the how-tos, let's examine the science-based frameworks that I use to support my clients in developing their emotional intelligence. In the past twenty years, there has been a great deal of research conducted on the interplay between the mental and emotional processes that we all engage in as we move through the world. As our knowledge of the physiological and neuro-circuitry of emotions has improved, so have the tools that can help you understand and manage your emotions more effectively. Let's explore three of the theoretical foundations that I use to frame what can sometimes feel like a minefield: 1. the Goleman and Bar-On models for EQ; 2. four major categories of unconscious bias; and 3. self-determination theory and the SCARF model.

"Emotional intelligence" came into common parlance with Daniel Goleman's book on the subject in the mid-1990s, but as far back as the early '80s, psychologists such as Reuven Bar-On, John Mayer, and Peter Salovey had been conducting research that assessed the brain's capacity for processing and managing emotions. To a certain extent, Goleman's work reinserted emotions back into a culture that had become uncomfortable with the feeling side of being human but was beginning to recognize that most major decisions made in the name of "logic" nonetheless have a strong emotional component.

It's ironic that from the early twentieth century through the 1970s and '80s, the ideal of leadership was focused on analytical intellectual ability. Characteristics such as charisma and extroversion were considered desirable but detached from emotional qualities; you either had them or you didn't. Fortunately, with the demise of the bureaucratic "manager" and the emergence of Bill Gates, Steve Jobs, and other entrepreneurs who emphasized creativity and inspiration, psychologists have come to recognize that charismatic behavior and communicating with feeling are qualities that anyone can develop.

Unfortunately, we generally still operate under the assumption that cognitive intelligence and emotional intelligence are separate (even though the value of "IQ" itself is controversial). Perhaps one day we will reach a deeper understanding of the integrated nature of human consciousness, and neural network studies are moving us in this direction. The good news is that the work of Goleman, Bar-On, and others has brought the value of emotions back onto the playing field. Sometimes, they're the most important factor of all.

Self-Awareness Redux: This Time with Feeling

Dan Goleman's framework starts at the same point that we used earlier to assess our cognitive approach to curiosity, listening, and directive versus consensus-driven behaviors: self-awareness. What is different is a focus on our own emotional states—how aware we are of our reactions and their impact on others. Observing ourselves, such that we can articulate what upsets or energizes us at any given moment, is almost antithetical to our culture (ironic in the age of the selfie). But there is a big difference between self-interest and self-knowledge. It is always easier to judge others than to look in the mirror, own our own feelings—good, bad, and indifferent—and seek to regulate an emotional terrain that often feels out of our control.

Goleman's framework divides emotional intelligence, or EQ, into two categories, one with an internal focus, the other external: 1. self-awareness and regulation of your own feelings; and 2. social awareness and regulation of how you interact with others. That is, to be an effective leader, we must be able to label and express the feeling side of our nature, and to read and respond to the feelings of others.

Let's start with four questions:

1. **Self-awareness:** Can you accurately identify your own emotions and tendencies as they happen?

2. **Social awareness:** Can you accurately identify the emotions and tendencies of others as you interact?

3. **Self-management:** Can you manage your own emotions and behavior to a positive outcome?

4. **Relationship management:** Can you manage any interaction you have with others constructively and to a positive outcome?

Thoughts and Feelings, Together Again

The model developed by Israeli psychologist Reuven Bar-On, known as the EQ-i 2.0, considers EQ to represent the integration of emotional and social capabilities that directly impact behavior.[2] What's particularly insightful about the Bar-On framework is that it comes as close as we get to collapsing the silos of cognition and emotion, knitting back together intellectual and affective processes to recognize the value of each and how much they rely on each other in leadership dynamics—decision-making, conflict management, team constructs, and so on. Bar-On recognizes that emotions are directly connected to success when it comes to our capacities for stress tolerance, reality testing, and problem-solving. What's great about this is it starts to break down the false wall—which goes all the way back to Plato—that would have us separate IQ from EQ. While all dimensions in the EQ-i 2.0 assessment are important, studies with more than two hundred thousand executives across the globe indicate that there are five qualities that repeatedly show up in effective leaders.

1. **Self-regard:** The capacity to accurately evaluate ourselves, which can lead to accepting and respecting ourselves. Respecting ourselves means we like the way we are—all the good and bad and in between.

2. **Emotional self-awareness:** The ability to recognize our emotions and distinguish between them.

3. **Assertiveness / emotional self-expression:** The ability to express feelings and beliefs, and defend our rights in a nondestructive manner.

4. **Empathy:** Sensitivity to how and why people feel the way they do. Being empathetic is being able to emotionally read other people, which means picking up on emotional cues.

5. **Problem-solving:** Together with reality testing and flexibility, this forms the triad of adaptability, or survival of the fittest. Problem-solving means identifying and defining stumbling blocks and then implementing effective solutions.

What's immediately noticeable is that this short list doesn't include solely what we think of as emotional processes. Effective leaders connect the dots between how we think about our feelings and how we feel about our thoughts. The EQ-i 2.0 assessment helps us understand how well leaders navigate obstacles when they feel connected to or passionate about them, and acknowledges how rare it is for any of us to face a problem with a totally dispassionate stance. You can do all the data analysis you like, but if your boss doesn't trust you, how your solution lands will hinge on emotions, not logic.

Maybe even more useful is the assessment's emphasis on pragmatic actions that you can take. Just knowing you need to improve your EQ is not very helpful—in fact, it can be negatively reinforcing to learn that you lack empathy or need to be more sensitive: What do you do with this information? Feel bad about yourself? Self-awareness is the pivot, but moving into action on your EQ is what matters. Let's look at some real-life cases of growth opportunities and the action steps that worked for them.

Self-Critical Sally

We all know that self-critical voice that shows up to keep us humble and realistic, and hold our egos in check. When this internal voice cajoles you to be more disciplined and hold yourself to high standards, it's providing a positive service to your psyche. But if it is consistently harsh and critical, you may feel diminished or stymied by its recriminations. When my client Sally got a lower score in self-regard on her EQ-i assessment, I asked whether she thought that was an accurate assessment of how she viewed herself.

A marketing manager at an e-commerce start-up, Sally was competent, and well-liked and respected by her colleagues. But during our coaching session she confided that she often felt insecure, with a long-running tape in her head, as she called it, that questioned her proficiency. For as long as she could remember, she struggled with feeling inadequate, and worked hard to keep her self-doubt under wraps by projecting a persona of confidence. Trouble was, the ruse was exhausting.

As is often the case with people with lower self-regard scores, Sally was generally fine with her subordinates; she overcame her sense of self-doubt by connecting with and mentoring junior staff, which reinforced her sense of competence. She generally felt comfortable with her peers as well. It was when she had to manage upward that the critical voice became debilitating. She struggled with presentations to senior executives, dealing with any kind of disagreement with her boss, or speaking up in conversations about her future. She was aware of how this might hold her back, but it was a revelation to consider it as part of her developmental path in the context of emotional intelligence, and she hadn't thought about what steps she might take (beyond psychotherapy to dig into her childhood traumas) to overcome or mitigate the effects of this internal chatter. When I shared these practices that could help her build self-confidence, she was game.

1. Create a strengths list, and ask at least five people to weigh in.

2. Choose one strength and make an action plan for leveraging it.

3. Define what higher self-regard would look like: What would be different if you had higher self-esteem?

4. Develop a daily gratitude practice. Studies have shown that people who actively experience gratitude for specific aspects of their life tend to have a more positive outlook.

Lost Larry

When I met with Larry to discuss his EQ-i results, I knew this entire exercise would be a challenge for him. A software engineer, Larry had an introverted personality and was not prone to dramatic expressions—either positive or negative. In fact, his steady demeanor was one of the reasons he had been promoted. Viewed as consistent and calm, he had developed a reputation as a reliable corporate citizen. On the other hand, as he aspired to take on leadership roles, he was not surprised to hear that an inability to articulate his feelings might one day prove problematic. He could be difficult to read and easily perceived as opaque, even uninspiring. Perhaps more important, he found it difficult to read *himself,* which showed up as having to "think" about his feelings before he could comfortably name them.

There's a reason why emotional self-awareness and emotional self-expression are juxtaposed on the EQ-i assessment: The former bleeds into the latter. As you might imagine, being able to articulate your own feelings is the starting point for recognizing what's going on for others. Larry confided that one of the challenges he felt as he took on a leadership role was his discomfort with some of the team members who were, as he put it, "a bit dramatic." My translation was that his discomfort with his own feelings had led him to be uncomfortable around others who exhibited theirs. Like with Sally, the starting point was recognizing how this EQ dimension might become an obstacle to Larry's future success, and then committing to actions that would help him develop his emotional musculature.

The key steps for anyone who struggles with awareness of his feelings at any given moment is to expand his vocabulary. Here are steps for reflection to grow your emotional self-awareness:

1. Keep a journal of your moods. Commit to spending a few minutes each day writing out your emotional ups and downs. The more you can put your feelings into words, the more comfortable you will become with them.

2. Grab a thesaurus and keep a running list of words that describe your feelings. Go beyond "happy," "sad," and "upset" to more nuanced expressions: "joyful," "glum," "morose," "triggered," "exasperated," "gleeful," "disappointed," "sorrowful," "grieving," "exuberant," "furious."

3. Make note of the feeling state you are in when you are most productive. What triggers that state? Make a commitment to do one thing that brings on that enthusiasm and focus every day.

4. Practice asking others how they are feeling, not just how they are doing. Then expand with probing questions: "What is your

gut reaction to this decision?" "What is your emotional response to this situation?"

Pushover Phil

As the chief operating officer of a large nonprofit, Phil had a reputation for being highly competent and respected by his colleagues. He often navigated conflicts between the sales, finance, and business strategy teams. As he put it, "There's nothing unusual about my having to play mediator; there is just a natural tension between some of those functions." In fact, the reason he moved up quickly from accounting clerk to finance manager to head of operations was because he is known as a diplomat.

Phil's EQ scores on many dimensions were high—he was strong on empathy, emotional awareness, self-expression, and interpersonal skills. But he came out lower on assertiveness. He told me, "That's not a surprise. The one thing that I often struggle with is standing up for myself. I've been told by bosses over the years that I need to take charge and make demands, but to be honest that feels counterintuitive to the way I've built my career. I worry that it might upset my colleagues if I come across as strident or self-aggrandizing."

Here we have the dilemma of a highly emotionally intelligent and successful leader who was stymied in his career by the very thing he does well. The questions for someone like Phil: How do you show up more assertively when appropriate, while still retaining your reputation as diplomatic and collegial? Are those competencies mutually exclusive?

I helped Phil experiment with deliberately taking stronger stands, speaking up, and connecting with his inner alpha. It felt risky at times, but he had nothing to lose, and if his colleagues noticed a change, he could always calm the waters by being transparent about what he was trying to do: grow as a leader.

Here are the action steps Phil took:

1. Identify your tolerance boundaries. When do you give in even when you disagree? When do you feel a sense of regret or disappointment because you caved in to the demands of others? What do you tolerate that you shouldn't?

2. List the trigger points that shut you down. They could be:
   - Lack of subject matter expertise
   - The presence of someone more senior
   - Lack of conviction
   - Facing off with strong personalities
   - Fear of disappointing or upsetting others

3. Practice assertive body language. For example, be attentive to your posture (sit up straight), lean in toward others when speaking, and maintain eye contact.

4. Describe a scenario in which you behaved assertively. What worked? Make a list and resolve to practice those same behaviors in a variety of circumstances. What was uncomfortable or less successful?

Whenever I work with a group using the EQ-i 2.0, I have them conduct this simple test: Go through the five dimensions listed on page 104 and rate yourself on a scale of one to five, one being an area you need to work on, five being a top strength. Better yet, show this list to colleagues or friends you trust and ask them to rate you on the same scale. When I ask my clients to self-test and then receive their actual assessment results, they are often not far off—a good indicator that many of us are already aware of our soft spots. If you are not sure where to begin, look at where you're strongest (where you scored higher) and make a list of what specific actions you engage in often that reinforce the positive. The key to building EQ is to leverage your strengths, then be willing to acknowledge your challenge areas—and get to work.

Shortcuts and Short Circuits

In his bestselling book *Thinking Fast and Slow,* Nobel Prize–winning psychologist and Princeton professor Daniel Kahneman explains that our decision-making processes occur in two modes: automatic and deliberate. He coined the terms "system one" and "system two" to describe how our cognitive processes are designed to maximize the energy the brain needs by making repeated ongoing decisions so routine that we don't even notice them. Think about driving a car (system one—an incredibly complex set of snap judgments that we barely notice) while also making a difficult decision (system two). This split-brain dynamic helps explain how easily we can go on autopilot, especially with habituated activities and thoughts: It saves energy. Kahneman's theory is rapidly replacing the heretofore accepted notion that our brains operate as right/left; scientists generally agree that the brain is much more complex than "right" as creative and intuitive, and "left" as rational.[3]

Yet, as Kahneman points out, there is a downside to a system-one focus on efficiency and saving energy: Even the most well-intentioned shortcuts can lead to short circuits, blind spots, and faulty reasoning. It's amazing how quickly choices that deserve system-two focus become system-one routinized, and our brains, in an attempt to save energy and protect us from danger, hurl us down the neural highway in a driverless vehicle that ends up parking in a cognitive cul-de-sac. That means stereotypes, gross generalities, unexamined beliefs, and faulty decision-making, whether the tired trope is "Women are more emotional than men" or "He went to the same school as me, so we should hire him."

Let's look back at that exchange between my client Joseph and his two direct reports, Michael and Rachel. Joseph was taken aback when I suggested that his assessment of their behavior might be tainted by unintentional gender bias. Asked to define what he considered to be "emotional" behavior, he quickly came around when I pointed out that what he was describing—higher-pitched tone of voice, manic or dramatic physical gestures, becoming red-faced, employing strong language—mapped *particularly to the male* protagonist of the mini-drama that we witnessed in his office. It was a tough pill to swallow, but it went down more easily when I told him about my own wake-up call to the ubiquity of gender-based bias and white male privilege.

One semester when I was in grad school, most of my classes had around twenty-four students, half men and half women. One day, a female classmate announced that she had been feeling repeatedly shut down by the tendency, as she put it, of the men to "dominate the conversation." Initially, we guys all balked, responding somewhat in unison, "We don't hog the dialogue. You are free to speak up as much as you like!" A few days later, however, that same student stood up in the middle of a mildly contentious debate—in which she was struggling to be heard—and shared data she had been collecting for weeks, noting down the number of times men spoke up versus women during class discussions. The difference was astounding (to the men in the room, at least): Something like 70 percent of the men participated but only 30 percent of the women. I felt guilty about having shouted her down in the first place, and humbled by my own complicity in reinforcing an unconscious cultural trope.

It was true: The men spoke up much more. We had assumed that our "mansplaining" was completely innocent; not true. As humbling as this experience was personally, it also emboldened me to develop the courage to speak truth to power in similar situations, rather than remain silent and thereby reinforce a false narrative and stereotype. The good news is that Joseph, an insightful and compassionate leader, was contrite and open to reconsidering his judgment. He also vowed to store my top ten list, which we will cover shortly, in his wallet to keep him "on his toes."

You Don't Know What You Don't Know

When it comes to unconscious bias, or implicit bias, there's good news and bad news. The good news is that bias in decision-making is garnering increased attention from psychologists, behavioral economists, and neuroscientists, who have come to recognize that even the most self-aware among us regularly fall headlong into the trap of making biased decisions. The bad news is that since the drivers of these decisions are unconscious, likely based on a combination of genetics, cultural input, and early childhood influences, it's well-nigh impossible for us to completely rid ourselves of these patterns. What we *can* do is to seek out methods to track ourselves and incorporate practices to unearth and address the culprit before it leads us down the garden path.

Many of these forms of bias are interrelated and show up in combinations. David Rock at the NeuroLeadership Institute, along with other researchers, have combed through the long list of common biases and separated them into broad categories. For the most part, these mental and emotional shortcuts tend to fall under four major headings:

1. **Information overload:** In today's information-inundated world, there is often just too much for us to process as we consider a choice. Hence, our efficient brains sort out the wheat from the chaff, quickly focusing on the data that seems to matter. "Seems to matter," however, is the rub. That tends to be that which is most familiar ("Many of my friends went to that school, so it must be high-quality"), related to a recent or personal experience ("Volkswagen is the best car; I've always driven a Volkswagen"), or can be easily assimilated and understood.

2. **Lack of information:** Sometimes, we simply do not have enough quality information to make an effective decision. When the narrative threads don't come together to form a complete picture, our system-one, quick-hit brain will fill in the gaps, based on previous experience. ("I had to drive in L.A. once, and now I avoid driving in cities.") This shows up in multiple forms, all of which tend to include making false connections, adding extraneous data for the sake of continuity, and linking familiar themes.

3. **Sense of urgency:** The third type of bias shows up when time is a factor or we feel a sense of urgency. We may prefer to leisurely sift through all the data, but in today's fast-paced business environment, that's often unrealistic. When time is of the essence, leaders are often evaluated on their ability to act. We tend to skip over information that might trip us up or require more deliberation. ("We should sign the contract now because the salesperson says this price is only available until midnight. We can always read the full contract later.") Likewise, we want to avoid ambi-

guity and seek clarity. ("Both candidates seem qualified, but let's just go with Steve. I struggle with pronouncing Amarazi's name.")

4. **Generalizations:** This fourth bucket can derail any of us, as our brains prefer efficiency over accuracy. As Kahneman points out, the motivation of system one is to minimize cognitive exertion, supposedly saving up ammunition for some major foe just around the corner. We extrapolate what "feels" most relevant, and avoid deeper analysis of the specifics or the unique character of a situation or person—which may be energy efficient, but comes at a price. ("I won't visit Paris anymore. My friend got mugged there once. Sad to think that it is no longer safe.")

When there is a surfeit of information, not enough information, we need to act quickly, or we rely on a generalization, our brain will drive us to make decisions that are often less than optimal. With all these cognitive land mines, what is a leader to do?

All the researchers agree that catching your own blind spots is almost impossible. In fact, self-monitoring creates a paradox: You just don't know what you don't know. Without some form of feedback, it's almost impossible to catch yourself, especially when your aware mind is in the back seat, while unconscious bias drives the bus. On the other hand, as I said, there is good news: In a group dynamic, we can build in practices that raise our collective awareness.

One example comes from the "council method" used for thousands of years by indigenous groups across the North American continent. Their wise leaders may not understand a concept like unconscious bias, but they know that blind spots, prejudice, personal agendas, and political rivalries often get in the way of decisions that impact the entire society. In these tribal councils, whenever there is a big decision to be made, the elders—the C-suite, as it were—sit in a circle while everyone figuratively steps into one another's shoes. The eldest member may take on the role of the youngest; a new mother, the chief; a warrior, the healer. Within this playacting dynamic, the group listens to arguments for and against the decision, from a range of perspectives. This is the type of lateral, instead of literal, thinking, that leads to better, less biased outcomes.

The Top Ten

Taking these four categories as a starting point, I've developed a method you can use to coach yourself and your team to stop unconscious bias in its tracks. The theme of this top-ten list is "all bias all the time." Whenever colleagues come together for a brainstorming session or to consider a major decision, I recommend they close the session by taking a few extra minutes to talk through the following list, asking themselves, with humor and candor: Have we been caught in any of the following?

INFORMATION OVERLOAD

1. **Literalizing:** Are we taking our data literally, not seeing metaphors and analogies but "just the facts"? Are we asking what might be missing? Are we employing lateral thinking as we examine this situation?

2. **Lost (in the woods):** Haven we fallen in love with our data, or are we seeing the bigger picture? Are we missing the forest for the trees?

3. **Lazing:** Are we luxuriating in our abundance of information? Are we being cavalier or dismissive because we feel like we

know enough that we don't need to investigate further? Are we picking and choosing what "feels" important and what happens to jump out at us?

TOO LITTLE INFORMATION

4. **Linking:** Are we linking stories together just to fill in the gaps? Are we making up connections that have no basis in fact but feel good and make the narrative add up?

5. **Loafing:** Are we focusing only on the information that's readily available, or most recent, or most acceptable because it matches what we already know? Are we taking time to review contrary opinions and data? Are we exploring all sides of an issue?

URGENCY/NEED TO ACT QUICKLY

6. **Lunging:** Are we lunging forward, dismissing or leaving out important information? Are we cutting to the chase?

7. **Leaving:** Who or what are we leaving behind? Are we taking the time to include everyone and everything that needs to be considered to arrive at a complete picture? Are we being inclusive or exclusive?

GENERALIZATIONS

8. **Liking:** Are we focused on what we like or don't like (in-group and out-group bias)? Are we recognizing when we "like" a decision because we "like" the people making it? Are we

focusing our attention on people who are like us, or are we open to people who are different?

9. **Lumping:** Are we lumping together data and people that have a superficial connection (stereotyping)? Have we used the terms "always" or "never," or other black-and-white phrases?

10. **Lingering:** Are we generalizing about our approach to a decision based on past experience? Are we focused on doing something because we have "always done it this way"? Are we making the common mistake of believing that what happened before will happen again?

In putting together the list, I had two goals: to make it accessible and easy to remember; and to ensure that anyone could connect with each item, no matter their background, sex, or culture (assuming fluency in English and knowledge of Western norms). Whenever unconscious bias trips us up, there are typically emotions—not data or logic—underpinning and driving the process. Remember: The elephant runs the show! We tend to feel first, think later. Decisions made only from "intuition" or by "following our gut" tend to indicate system one in action. I have found that having a simple list of questions that have an almost instant emotional resonance to them can be helpful in bringing our attention to places where unconscious bias may be lurking.

Loving the List

I recommend that my clients post this list somewhere handy to be referenced after a decision-making or brainstorm session. If you are the leader and comfortable with yourself as a role model, an important starting point for raising everyone's awareness of unconscious bias is to acknowledge, with humility and humor, that you are biased, as is everyone in the room. That creates an ambience of safety so that the team can reflect on the questions with each L-word and unearth possible areas of bias without judgment or acrimony. The team can even have fun with the list, and nip prejudice in the bud to make better decisions.

When I introduce the top ten at development or brainstorming meetings with clients, I'll start by asking them to quickly go through the list and share any examples that come to mind. Take a moment to read back through the list and see if you can think of a situation where one of these L-words was lurking beneath your decision. We all want to do the right thing and feel good about it, but we must first be reflective and honest with our compatriots, and with ourselves.

Self-Determination Theory (SDT) and SCARF

Let's turn to two recent developments in the science of emotions and motivation that have expanded the toolkit for leaders to foster high-performance teams: self-determination theory, or SDT, and the SCARF model.

Self-determination theory, developed by psychologists Edward Deci and Richard Ryan at the University of Rochester, has demonstrated that there are three core themes that underpin human motivation: autonomy, relatedness, and competence. "Autonomy" refers to our ability to make decisions for ourselves, to operate independently, and to work in an environment where our opinions and feelings are taken into consideration. "Relatedness" refers to the bonds of trust and interpersonal support that are foundational to our sense of belonging. A sense of "competence" is reinforced with regular feedback and encouragement to learn and grow. These three characteristics strongly impact the likelihood that individuals and teams will live up to their full potential.

It's a bit of a paradox that as the world gets smaller and technology enables twenty-four-hour connections, more people feel disconnected and even alienated from their work groups. In a world where more and more of us work from home, independently, or in virtual teams, research indicates that despite that distance, motivation still relates to a person's sense of connection, a feeling of being part of something bigger. This can be problematic for leaders hoping to maintain the sense of enthusiasm and motivation that is fueled by interpersonal relationships.[4]

Likewise, neuroscience research using fMRI studies of how the brain responds to external inputs indicates that these three dimensions can either trigger the brain's reward system or, when either neglected or negatively reinforced with punishment or fear-based communication, the threat-defense system—fight or flight. The latter, unsurprisingly, fosters a downward spiral of territoriality, competition, and mistrust.

Those fMRI studies of network activity in the brain have also provided substantial data on two additional salient factors: status and fairness. If you have ever felt a twinge of irritation at hearing about the elevation of someone you deem unworthy (even though you admit you don't have all the data) or a bit of pique when someone else wins a prize in a raffle (especially if you bought a ticket, too!), then you are well acquainted with the brain's reaction to perceived slights when it comes to status or fairness.

Reflecting that knowledge, the model developed by David Rock at the NeuroLeadership Institute is called SCARF (status, certainty, autonomy, relatedness, and fairness). Understanding them as primary needs helps us better navigate the social aspects of the workplace.[5] To explore how these emotion-driven motivators show up in the real world, let's look at an example where many of these factors converged, in an initially detrimental way.

Harsh Hannah

Hannah was the senior program manager for a division of clinical trial scientists, where she had a reputation for being assertive, action oriented, and results focused. Her team ran like clockwork, maintaining timetables, setting deadlines, tracking results. She was well-liked by her physician and scientist colleagues, who worked in a research lab on behalf of large pharmaceutical firms sponsoring clinical trials. Hannah's team of twelve project managers had a reputation for diligence, discipline, and focus.

The trouble started when she received confidential feedback from her subordinates. All the positive feedback about her team's diligence seemed to come with a price, for Hannah also had a reputation for being intolerant of mistakes and demanding to the point of harshness.

When her empathy score came back somewhat lower than her other emotional intelligence dimensions on the EQ-i 2.0 assessment, I wasn't surprised. "I'd love to have tons of empathy for my people, but my job doesn't lend itself to feel-good hugging circles," she said, responding to the results with a laugh. "This is a tough job. I manage the staff who track projects both for the client and the researchers. If we get behind, we lose money. Empathy is something that I save for the weekends with my kids—if am soft on my people at work, we could all be out of a job!"

SCARF, SDT, and the Will to Change

Hannah's team was a classic millennial group: educated, motivated, and committed. But it seemed no matter how much direction she gave, including setting goals and time parameters, and providing guidance on client interactions, as soon as she was back in her office, they would devolve into gossip and, as she saw it, laziness.

I suggested that I meet with each member of Hannah's team, just to listen. It was immediately obvious that many of their concerns were directly connected to those five dimensions of motivation. They complained about Hannah's micromanagement, her lack of availability ("Her office is too far away"; "She is distant"; "She is rarely visible"), and an approach that was more punitive than supportive. Given our earlier discussions about empathy, I wasn't entirely surprised to hear these complaints. What was surprising and added a level of complexity to the group dynamic were their complaints about one another.

Some of them said that their job titles were not commensurate with their level of competence; some said that since their colleagues were lazy, they felt unmotivated, saying, "What's the point of putting in hard work if the person sitting right next to me is always on Facebook?" Others complained about a clique that had formed in the office, leaving them feeling "on the outs," and making the overall dynamic feel like a high school cafeteria. One of the more senior staff remarked, "We're just cogs in the machine here. When we see Hannah coming down the hall with the whip, it feels like we're in the nineteenth century. We know when she is on the warpath, so we quickly clam up and hide out. It wasn't always this way, but these days I barely trust anyone on the team."

We had here a group of talented, educated people that in most circumstances would strive to do their best, support one another, and look to improve personally and as an organization. Yet they were going exactly in the opposite direction. Hannah's supposed lack of empathy was clearly one factor, but the question remained: Since she tended to manage at arm's length and grant them a certain amount of autonomy, how to account for the disempowerment and infighting? The team context itself needed to be addressed. As the SCARF model would indicate, a threat response was clearly being triggered, with issues of status and fairness front and center.

Once Hannah and I had an opportunity to discuss the situation, it became clear that the first thing she needed to do was somewhat counterintuitive. She had been accused of being a micromanager, but there was a lot of contradictory feedback related to her day-to-day engagement with the team. The only way to reveal the truth would be to literally get closer, at least temporarily, so she moved her office down the hall and started working in her team's midst, at first much to their chagrin.

Secondly, she needed to take an inventory of the gifts, talents, and strengths of her people. Hannah met with each one of them, not to discuss what was going wrong or to collect complaints, but to talk through their talents and what was possible in their roles. She prompted them to think about how they could grow: Where did they see themselves a year down the road? How could their current role—with Hannah's support—get them there? As a final shift, Hannah instituted an informal mentoring program, encouraging each of the junior staff to buddy up with a more seasoned member of the team.

These were all great steps, but there was still one dimension from the SCARF framework that Hannah had left out of the mix: *certainty*. One of the cultural dynamics of the office that had fostered insecurity stemmed from an unspoken understanding that project management was less important than the work of the scientists and researchers. In a typical tech or science-focused environment, I have found that it is not unusual for "nonessential" functions (which absolutely *are* essential) to sometimes be treated as second-class citizens. It was extremely unlikely that Hannah's organization could even operate without project management, but there was always a possibility that some of these roles would be automated as PM software improved and became more user-friendly. On the other hand, that likelihood was minimal. But the fear factor was very real, and this underlying vibe of uncertainty was having a destructive impact on morale. With that in mind, Hannah took one more step: She started inviting team members to join update meetings with senior management on a rotating basis. In these meetings, her team members got visibility and exposure to just how important project management was to the C-suite, which assuaged their fears and bolstered morale.

The SDT and SCARF models can be extremely helpful for leaders who fail to account for intrinsic motivators and cognitive triggers that can cause even high-functioning individuals to behave in counterproductive ways. When Hannah focused her efforts on building on her team's individual strengths and fostering a sense of fairness and belonging, the dissatisfied band of underlings that I had first encountered roared back into a successful team with renewed enthusiasm and a sense of possibility.

Bifurcation Bias

Before we dive deeper into the emotional facets of leadership, stop for a moment and reflect on what we've touched on so far. Do you notice any overarching theme or motif? If not, not to worry. I didn't either—until I took a step back. What I saw was a bit shocking: It appears that all our evidence-based frameworks for ways of thinking, feeling, and being as leaders tend to bifurcate into either-or categories: extrovert versus introvert, emotional versus cognitive intelligence, system-one versus system-two thinking, even alpha versus beta (my own categories!)—not to mention the familiar trope of the left versus right brain, which splits our creative and intuitive capabilities from analytic processes.

Recent research conducted by Richard Boyatzis and his colleagues at Case Western University seems to point to yet another binary understanding of our cognitive powers: task versus relationship. Task versus relationship appears to be another shortcut to help us navigate the world efficiently, in this case, with task-oriented, directive behavior favored over relationship-building approaches. We can understand why we may have historically tended to create those sorts of silos: The more efficient our focus, the more likely we were to survive. Collaboration and consensus take time and energy. But the opposite is also true. Human progress has almost always been more evident within communities with a strong sense of familial cohesion and social ties. Humans are consummate social animals—our success as a species is directly connected to our ability to work together and foster belonging.[6]

Our goal today must be to transcend the gap between these taskmaster versus relationship builder divisions. Our evolution depends upon us seeing through antiquated, polarized constructs such as task/relationship, emotions/thoughts, introvert/extrovert, masculine/feminine, alpha/beta, lest we forget that they all come from the same place: between our ears.

Be Emotional: From IQ to EQ and Beyond

The starting point for developing emotional intelligence, or EQ, is to recognize your emotional style. This is not about being "emotional" per se, it's about being tuned in and recognizing habitual patterns. One of the lessons I learned early in my career as a psychologist was that when emotions run high in relationships—personal and professional—we all have patterns that emerge. There are two categories that I frequently encounter in the workplace: the turtle and the octopus.

Sarah was in her early thirties, a rising star as a human resources manager at a global financial services firm, but struggling with Pete, her peer on the HR team. Their boss, the head of HR, was at his wits' end: While they cooperated while managing within their silos—Sarah focused on recruiting, Pete on training—when there was overlap, while assimilating new hires for instance, things would get heated. Sarah and Pete had fallen into a classic pattern: You do your work, I do mine; let's grab lunch and be collegial, but let's not collaborate if we can avoid it! Whenever there was an important opportunity, sparks would fly: Who was in charge? Who would control the junior staff? Who would get the credit when things went well, or, more to the point, the blame if things went awry?

When their boss asked me to play mediator, I brought Sarah and Pete together, with smartphones set aside for a full fifty minutes. The octopus-turtle dynamic was immediately evident. Pete, reluctant to enter what to him felt like unnecessary "couples counseling," was clearly a turtle, withdrawing whenever confronted with difficult questions. The irony of this behavior was that it was the opposite of how Sarah had described him: extroverted, alpha, and social. She viewed him as dominant in the relationship, and herself as the more sensitive, more submissive colleague, whose needs always took second place. But I watched a different emotional dance play out. When strong emotions were involved, the power dynamic between their styles reversed. Sarah was more verbal and even physically assertive— leaning in, gesturing broadly, becoming flush with emotion. The more Pete retreated—eyes downcast, leaning back, arms folded in his lap—the more she moved in, probed with questions, launched into diatribes about how she was just trying to get work done, a classic octopus in action. Sarah was surprised to learn that she took on an alpha stance when the stakes were high. Pete, meanwhile, was a strong presence, and I could imagine him being quite directive with his staff, but his response to emotional confrontation was to shut down.

Coaching the two of them was relatively straightforward from there. Pete was aware that he shut down but didn't know what to do about it. When I suggested that he might need to work on building up a more robust vocabulary for his emotions, and request time to process his feelings, it all clicked into place. He clearly had strong emotions during the conversation but felt oppressed by Sarah's intensity. In the tangle of her "octopus" arms, Pete was overwhelmed, unable to sort through his feelings. Likewise, Sarah was unaware of how domineering she could become, and Pete's uncharacteristic retreat, which made her feel unheard, sent her into an even more assertive outburst.

Sarah and Pete broke out of their negative spiral. The key to their success was learning how the other responded to emotional triggers. So, are you an octopus or a turtle?

1. When you are upset about something, do you want to "handle" it right away? (Octopus.)

2. When you have negative feelings, do you sometimes struggle to find words that match the emotions? (Turtle.)

3. When you feel anger or disappointment, do you tend to want to "get it out of your system"? (Octopus.)

4. When confronted with an upset colleague, do you look to escape as quickly as possible? (Turtle.)

Turtles and octopuses, it turns out, are just the beginning. My Institute of Coaching colleague Susan David, who wrote the brilliant book *Emotional Agility*, describes two other patterns that people often employ when emotions run high: bottlers and brooders. Bottlers avoid feeling their feelings, lacking a vocabulary to help clarify what may feel like a flood of emotions. Brooders tend to ruminate and hold on to feelings long after they have any benefit or impact, processing a situation with self-recrimination or holding a grudge against others. Many of us toggle back and forth depending upon the circumstance.

As Susan points out, these patterns likely develop early in our lives when we either witness how authority figures express or avoid emotions, or are told directly what to do with our feelings. If, as a child, Pete was told not to cry at his grandfather's funeral ("Have a stiff upper lip; don't upset Mommy"), he may have developed a bottler/turtle pattern early on. Likewise, Sarah's tendency to allow her emotions to build until they released with a bang is a classic brooder pattern that she may have either witnessed or been encouraged to take up as a child.

As children, we develop defensive strategies to help cope with uncomfortable or "inappropriate" feelings. These defense mechanisms come in a variety of forms, but they all have one thing in common: They protect us from a challenging world. Children need love and acceptance—they can't survive, let alone thrive, on their own. Strategies for coping with emotions are key to successful development; they help us form a strong ego, or, put another way, a sense of self and esteem, so we can operate in a complex world filled with mixed signals.

Later in life, however, these same patterns can become liabilities. As leaders, it is unhelpful to be stuck in any paradigm that undermines our effectiveness in working with others. With practices like mindfulness, as we discussed in chapter 3, we can become observers of our own tendencies, and from there we can expand to a new level of awareness and coach ourselves with fresh practices to build greater strength and flexibility in our emotional musculature.

By now you may be thinking, "Wow, this is a minefield!" And to a certain extent you'd be right—emotional patterns are complex and deep—but rest easy. Just as with your leadership style or your communication style, once you have a sense of your unique combination of behavior around emotions, you can begin to implement a strategy that will lead to greater effectiveness and less wasted energy. In short, you can coach yourself, using Susan's three-step process for "unhooking" from strong emotions: 1. Label your thoughts and emotions; 2. Accept them; and 3. Act on your values (and not your feelings).

To get a sense of how this works in the real world, let's look at a few leaders and how becoming aware of their emotional patterns helped them reframe their options. See if you can recognize yourself.

The Cerebral Alpha

As the director of the clinical research group at a nonprofit institute, an MD and cardiologist by training, Steve was a classic alpha leader. He tended to be strong willed and directive, and, in keeping with his training, have an authoritative, if jovial, demeanor. Whenever things got a bit heated with his staff—a minor conflict about timetables for a client study, for example—his emotional style was what you might expect: He leaned in, spoke forcefully, and tended to use words that sounded rational—but as they came out faster and louder, his emotions came to the surface, too. Steve treated everyone fairly, stuck with the data, and tended to steer clear of more personal topics, with an "all work all the time" approach. He was also good at lightening up a tense moment with a self-deprecating story or joke. He struck me at first as an equal-opportunity alpha octopus.

But, as a few of his staff members shared with me, his style, despite the flashes of humor, could come across as harsh and intimidating. For Steve, coaching meant learning to be more restrained and hold himself back when he felt triggered, and allowing time for others to process what he said. He also needed to watch his tone of voice, which tended to rise with his excitement level, and its pace, which tended to speed up whenever things got intense. It was a revelation for him to realize that even though what he was saying was rational and reasonable, when the topic became emotionally charged, he got loud and forceful, making even other alphas on his team recoil and shut down—the opposite of what he intended.

Breaking the habits we all develop over many years takes practice. To ensure Steve's success, I suggested he keep a couple of touchstones strategically positioned to help catch himself in the octopus act. The first was a slogan that exemplified his core values when it came to conflict: "win-win-win." He had this carved into a wood block that he placed in the center of the conference table in his office—an omnipresent reminder to him (and to anyone) that the goal was always to find a resolution that worked for everyone. The second touchstone, "Keep Calm and Carry On," he posted on his computer screen—a well-known British tagline from World War II that reminded him to pause, stay grounded, and add extra time for listening whenever he felt strongly. It also brought levity and lightened Steve's mood.

The Emotional Alpha

Social, extroverted, and with a bigger-than-life personality, Beth was superb at her job as a director of operations for an international engineering firm. She loved networking and knew how to "work the room," as she would say, when the company entertained visitors and customers from Eastern Europe and other international locales. With a tendency to use humor to deflect tension between herself and her boss, which was not always appreciated, her attitude got her into trouble at times. When situations became emotionally charged, Beth had a reputation for running either hot or cold. Because she was known as a big talker with robust opinions on just about everything related to the organization's operations, whenever she felt that she was in the right, she quickly became an octopus, relentless in her quest to prove herself. Likewise, when she was less sure of an answer, she could at times flummox everyone around her by shutting down—turtle. Typically, as she told me, "If I don't know the answer, or where to find it, it's better for me to hold my tongue."

Beth was aware of her tendency to come on strong, and she knew how to use this to her organization's benefit. Her highly expressive nature worked well with clients and when she was called upon to defend her staff. Where she needed coaching was to develop a more consistent response to conflict, as she hurt her reputation with other senior leaders when she shut down; they viewed her as unpredictable and self-absorbed. She needed to learn to be okay with not always having the answer and to be curious, ask questions, and put forth options instead of withdrawing into her proverbial shell.

Following Susan's recipe for emotional agility, Beth began to practice pausing to name her gut reaction to a tense situation before speaking or shutting down. Her touchstone was a large Post-it note on her laptop that read "Name it to tame it!" Since she carried her laptop with her to most meetings, the note reminded her in the moment to reflect and calibrate before acting. Her core value turned out to be "Do the right thing." But she came to see that she didn't need to always have the answer; she could simply state that she didn't know!

The Somatic Alpha

Recognizing the somatic octopus is easy: He is the leader, who, even if small in stature, physically takes over a space when emotions are aroused. He gets up from the table and walks around the room, closing in on his interlocutors. (You may remember Donald Trump's looming, threatening performance during his debates with Hillary Rodham Clinton: His physical presence became as much a part of the dynamic as his words or gestures.)

My client Sidney was about five feet four inches tall, and normally ran his technology team with a quiet, unemotional demeanor. But when he felt strongly about an issue, or if there was a conflict on the horizon, his inner street fighter appeared out of nowhere. Multiple times, I saw him stand up, lean over a table, and get in the face of a colleague just to make a point, with no particular malice or ill will. The octopus would come alive. His colleagues, fortunately for him, were accustomed to this onslaught, so were not entirely shocked when Mr. Calm and Reserved suddenly loomed over them, face in a grimace. He had developed a reputation for being "prickly" and "getting on his soap box" (almost literally whenever he would stand up and pound the table). His colleagues attempted to avoid conflict by "managing" him, which is never ideal.

Coaching Sidney required him to become much more aware, in the moment, of his tendency to allow his feelings to take over; he needed to tame the octopus. During one brainstorming session with him and his team, I had the opportunity to see Sidney's rather understated persona transform before my eyes. Suddenly he was up out of his chair, circling the room, speaking loud and fast, hovering over one of his staff, with a tone that dripped condescension. Later, in a one-on-one feedback session, he was contrite. "It was certainly not my intent to shut down the conversation," he reflected, "but I guess I did get a bit up in Cary's face. Sometimes I just get crazy when the team doesn't understand what I'm trying to accomplish."

I did my best to stick with the specifics of the behavior I observed. When I posed the question of values—what Sidney intended as an outcome for these kinds of discussions—he was quick to respond: "I want to bring out the best ideas to get to the best solution."

His wake-up call, I suggested, was to recognize that bringing out the best in others might require him to be more restrained, to manage his passion, and to remember that the "best minds" include the minds of others, not just his own! Sidney came to understand that during any potential conflict, he would tend to revert to a childhood tactic: "I would always go at the potential troublemaker first. I had to make up for being small by being brave. Otherwise, as I remember all too well, I would get beaten up. Better to fight first and win."

Those childhood tactics had worked, protecting him from bullies, but that very same defense strategy was now working against him, unknowingly turning him into a bully himself. His signature strengths had become a liability—he was no longer a street kid who needed to survive the schoolyard. He laughed when I used the metaphor of a male peacock, and acknowledged that his expansive plumage would sometimes pop out at inopportune moments. Once Sidney became aware of how his physical reaction to tension undermined his own values, he, like Beth and Steve, practiced restraining himself, both emotionally and physically. I recommended that he develop a somatic practice that would keep him connected to his body at times when he felt his pulse quicken: He would sit on his hands, stay seated, and force himself to sit up straight (leaning back or with arms crossed might send the wrong signal). It didn't come easily, but as he reminds me every time I see him, "I'm doing my best to stay 'in the box' instead of getting on top of it!"

The Cerebral Beta

On the other end of the spectrum from Sidney, we have a quintessential cerebral beta in Sam, a vice president of finance for a *Fortune* 100 consumer goods company. Cool, calm, and collected, Sam prided himself on being the adult in the room whenever things got emotional or there was conflict among his colleagues. When I had the opportunity to observe Sam, it wasn't immediately obvious what he needed to work on. On the one hand, he seemed relaxed and focused on listening to a debate about investing in a software application. Initially I took his emotional style and approach as quintessential beta—he listened well, was engaged and focused, and sought compromise—all of which would demonstrate his ability to bring out the best in his team.

Yet when I had an opportunity to query a couple of his subordinates, although they acknowledged that Sam's style had a calming effect—that he was generally diplomatic—they also confided that they had a hard time reading him. In one-on-one conversations, each had heard him voice strong opinions, so they were perplexed when in a team setting he would hold back, choosing to play ambassador. He is what I would call an *occasional* turtle. During emotionally charged debates, he would go into observer mode, which came across to others as disengagement.

I had witnessed him engage forthrightly with colleagues and, perhaps more important, with the CEO—his boss—so I knew that Sam did not lack vocabulary for his feelings. He told me that he sometimes held back because he wanted to hear people out before taking a stand, and he didn't want to overly influence the dialogue; he knew that coming from a power position, his opinion might undercut the candor of his team.

All of this made good sense and for the most part revealed Sam to be thoughtful and self-aware. But his diplomacy often left his colleagues feeling insecure or unmotivated. The bottom line is that his impressive emotional awareness was undercut by his demeanor, which projected distance, a lack of clarity, and even coldness. Sam needed to up the ante on his self-expression with tiny tweaks that would not just keep everyone connected and clear about his stand on any given subject, but also leave them feeling inspired.

I suggested that he consider simply paying closer attention to his body language. He often sat with arms crossed and an unexpressive facial expression, which made him difficult to read. I recommended leaning forward, uncrossing his arms, and smiling more. He laughed. "I didn't realize I wasn't smiling," he said. "I guess I always thought that my quiet, reserved stance shows up as smiling." I told him that we often think we're smiling when we're not. Even if he tried to de-emphasize his position, people pay attention when you're the boss. He may have wanted to remain neutral, but his team would try to read his body language and tone anyway.

To take his leadership to another level, Sam had to learn to remain present and enthusiastic, expressing himself both physically and verbally at appropriate moments, even if his intention was to listen. In this way, his impressive emotional agility would come to the fore.

The Emotional Beta

The whirlwind of energy and enthusiasm that Anne Marie exhibited in the first five minutes of our meeting was impressive, all while sipping her fourth Starbucks of the day (it was 11 A.M.). I knew right away that I was engaging with a highly passionate and highly intelligent leader of this sales team. At first, I mistook her for an extroverted alpha: decisive and opinionated. But as with all of us, her leadership and emotional styles were more complex than that.

When she shared the leadership agility assessment with her team, for the most part they rated her as beta. When I asked her about what appeared to be a contradiction between how she engaged with me and the way she had been perceived by her colleagues, she laughed it off. "I am a very strong personality," she said, "but I know how to behave with my team. I know how to keep my emotions in check, and listen before speaking. Part of what makes the sales team work effectively is that even when we have strong feelings, we set a tone of collaboration and listening. For the most part, we work toward consensus.

After all, I want to build a coaching culture into my team—we all need to support each other to succeed. I may let my hair down with you as my coach, but I'm self-tracking when it comes to interacting with my team, my peers, my boss."

"Bravo," I said. "You clearly have a sense of what it takes to navigate today's flatter leadership landscape."

"Yes," she replied. "Most of my team are millennials, and I'm not much older than them. We all want to feel like a community, that we are doing something meaningful and that we're aligned."

Anne Marie's colleagues had a slightly different story. Although they were generally impressed with her leadership style, they told me that at times she was "incredibly intense" and too easy to read, wearing her emotions on her sleeve. Even though she played the diplomat in public settings, they all knew when she was upset or felt strongly about something. They also knew to stay out of her way when she'd had too much coffee.

Anne Marie was a little shocked when I shared this feedback. Even though she knew she was highly emotional, she believed that she kept it under wraps. Like Sam, she was generally a successful beta leader, who worked well with her team. She needed only a few calibrations to her emotional agility to take her effectiveness to another level. She needed to pay closer attention, not just to how she was thinking about her feelings, but how she was acting or not acting on them. In short, she needed to pay attention to her body language: how she was moving through the office, how she was gesticulating, her facial expressions, the tone of her voice. At the end of the day, for a beta leader like Anne Marie, the bottom line was recognizing that less is more.

Making our way through the emotional landscape of today's professional environment can feel like trying to find a path in unmarked terrain. Gone are the old rules that bordered on an emotion ban in the office, with blanket prohibitions such as "Never cry at work." But how much emotion is appropriate? How much can you express before you seem unprofessional?

It's critical to become acquainted with your emotional style. Here are a few questions for reflection:

- Which of the leaders described most resonate with you? Why?
- If your colleagues were asked to describe your emotional style in one or two words, what would they say?
- What does being "emotionally expressive" mean to you?
- How would you characterize your default reaction when emotions run high?

Once you have a sense of your own style, the next step toward emotional agility is self-regulation. Here's where putting on your coach hat will be most useful. We all have our light and dark sides, and just like sunrise and sunset, they will flow through you with some regularity. The question is not whether you will experience intense emotions, but what you do with them, how you recognize them, and how you work with them toward productive ends.

Taming the Amygdala Hijack

Our next challenge is to develop practices to manage your emotions, as I did with Sidney and Beth. This is a lifelong challenge for all of us. In a world where subways get stuck, flights get delayed, and to-do lists seem endless, it is impossible to maintain a sense of balance at all times. At some point, we all fall victim to being reactive; we all get triggered.

In this same vein, those of us who tend to be more expressive, bringing good energy to most situations, may be prone to the "amygdala hijack." The amygdala is the part of the brain that controls our emotional responses, which show up almost instantaneously in physical form. Something catches you off guard and that smile and open posture transforms into a scowl, your shoulders tense. You're caught: hijacked.

No-Fault Fault Lines

To get a sense of how this amygdala hijack occurs in real time, let's review the scenarios I've shared in this chapter. No matter your emotional style, no one is immune to being triggered. The challenge is to become awake to what sets us off, to recognize the specific dynamics or environmental input that trips us up.

What transformed Steve, a rational alpha, into an intimidating octopus? As he told me, "It usually occurs when I feel like my colleagues are just not listening to me. I suddenly sense that I'm repeating myself, or notice that someone has gone off on an unrelated tangent that frustrates me." The actual trigger point may vary, but there is an underlying theme: He didn't feel heard.

Likewise, Beth started out exuberant and expressive, but sometimes something prompted her to go dark: She shut down, frowned, went silent. When I asked her what caused this shift, she said, "It feels like no one is listening to me. I can feel the conversation shifting in a direction where my opinion is either dismissed or ignored. My boss will hijack the conversation with her personal agenda, or sometimes a colleague will go on a rant, and I get so frustrated that I just want to pick up my toys and go play in a different sandbox."

Can you begin to see a pattern here? With both Steve and Beth, the precise trigger may have varied, but what played out was a narrative based on fear: *I am not being heard; I am being dismissed; I am not being taken seriously; everyone is against me.* All are twists on a deep-seated insecurity that many—maybe all—of us carry at some level: *I don't matter.* Whether it's feeling victimized or abandoned, impatient or frustrated, the story is the same. At some point in a perfectly well-intentioned interaction, some granular slight occurs, and our brain launches into protective mode. Neural circuits light up, cortisol and other stress hormones are released, and as we noted in chapter 5, in particularly sensitive domains—status, certainty, autonomy, relatedness, fairness, competence—emotional red flags start waving. We traverse the fault line, instantly redirecting our neural signals from system two to system one, and guess what? The theater of conscious action goes dark: We are no longer running the show.

There's no magic formula for preventing this, and it is important to give yourself a break, because we all get triggered. But it is possible to mitigate the impact and lessen the likelihood of being derailed. The key to success starts with self-awareness, to become your own seismograph, asking, "What is my fault line? What causes the volcano to erupt?"

Going forward, you can be your own coach by engaging in these five action steps.

Trigonometry of Triggers

The diagrams on the next page show the energetic paths we all follow when triggered. START represents the typical downward spiral: breakdown, conflict, upset. SSTTOOPP shows you how to work through those triggers and regain your emotional balance.

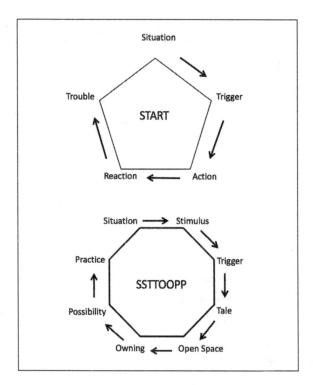

There are five steps to support you in building the capability and habit of "SSTTOOPPing," minimizing the pain of hijack:

1. **Draw up a pet peeve list:** What sets you off? What is triggering you is likely consistent and repetitive, and becoming aware of it is a great way to ward it off before it occurs. After living in the harried pace of New York City for years, I realized that I was easily frustrated by the lengthy small talk that occurs in slower paced towns (that is, just about everywhere else). Once I recognized that my revved-up energy was making me impatient and unfriendly, thus reinforcing the stereotype of the rude New

Yorker, I vowed to downshift my energy when I travel, to be more sensitive to my surroundings and collegial like a local.

2. **Look for cause and effect:** What is the "fear story" that is playing out in the background? When you are feeling calm, reflect on times when you have been triggered. Look to diagnose the underlying story or belief that drove the emotional eruption. As we discussed, typically some negative experience from the past reemerges in those moments. Psychologists note that people who, through no fault of their own, set us off often exhibit energy or behavior reminiscent of childhood drama or trauma (your boss may be like your dad; your coworker may have habits similar to a sister with whom you often quarreled as a child).

3. **Be gentle with yourself:** Can you accept your own humanity? We all get triggered. Be cautious of any tendency to become self-critical or defensive once you recognize that you've been set off; that exacerbates the pain. Better to acknowledge that you are not perfect—and apologize if necessary. You may be surprised how forgiving staff and colleagues will be once you own your foibles. Being vulnerable is a great way to role-model effective leadership in action.

4. **Create space:** Can you "pause" the action? The key to shifting your energy when triggered is to stop, breathe, and disconnect, even if just for a few moments. Take a quick walk around the block or a few deep breaths. It is important to get out of your head and into your body. Emotions always play out in physical form, so when the brain is hijacked, the body—by simple acts such as walking or stretching—will support you in creating space between your emotions and your actions.

5. **Refocus on values:** "What is my purpose in this situation? What do I most care about?" Reflect on your intentions and the inten-

tions of others. Generally, your staff or your colleagues are not trying to derail your day. Reconnecting to your fundamental values and trying to see from the perspective of others— practicing empathy—will help you reground, dissipate the fear energy, and get you back on track.

Bubble, Bubble, Toil and Trouble

When I first met Deborah, the director of operations for a global health nonprofit, I was impressed by her bubbly personality, her positive attitude, and her gracious interpersonal style. She seemed open to feedback and earnest in her desire to grow as a leader. Over coffee, she regaled me with stories of how much she loved her work, valued her colleagues, and had hustled to climb quickly into a leadership role—and, unlike many of my clients, Deb seemed very emotionally available.

She was also the only woman on the nonprofit's executive team. Feedback from superiors had been generally positive, so she was surprised to discover that I had been brought in because she had a reputation for being a bit tone-deaf. Her colleagues saw her as blunt and dismissive, with a tendency to use sarcasm and off-the-cuff humor to deflect anything that she deemed touchy-feely. She needed to become aware of her emotional self, not so that she could be more expressive, but so she could rein herself in.

To help her discover what she experienced as triggering, I had her create a "notepad for feelings" on her smartphone and start naming her emotional state in real time. Whenever she would emerge from a tumultuous meeting or an intense call, she got in the habit of taking a few seconds to ask herself, "What am I feeling?" Then she would add that word, or many, to her list: "confused," "disappointed," "frustrated," and so on. In the fraction of time it took to write down those words, she was often shocked to find that the feelings themselves would shift. I recommended that if there were a few extra minutes available, she open a thesaurus. Having a longer list of emotional descriptors was especially helpful for Deb to notice subtle shifts and nuances in her reactions. This EQ detective work started to broaden her self-perception. She came to recognize that she was more volatile than she had always thought.

Just taking a few moments to get clear on what she was feeling and note the differences between frustration, impatience, disappointment, anger, hurt, and sadness, for example, helped her see just how much variety she experienced in the space of a few minutes or hours. She came to note how certain colleagues would incite strong feelings in her. But what mattered most was that she also noticed how little time—maybe just a few deep breaths—was necessary to switch gears.

Once, she told me, "Earlier today, I had a tiff with a particularly irritating colleague, but with your advice in my head, I took a detour instead of barging into my next meeting all flustered and upset. I walked outside and around the building for two minutes, breathed in the sunshine. Then I stopped to jot down my feelings. I found myself smiling when I was looking up all the variations of my disdain for this person, and I went from pissed off to relaxed in a matter of moments."

She came to see how much more control she had over how she reacted and what she did with all the feelings that emerged. Once she took the time to reset her emotional barometer, she would do whatever she had to do to regain her sense of humor. "My team and I often laugh and get playful with each other when things are going well," she said. "Humor is a top value for me—I just need to make sure it is working for me, not against me."

Quick-Hit Workout: Alpha to Beta

1. **High point/low point:** Go back in five-year increments over your life and reflect on the highest and lowest moments: the most exciting, joyful, celebratory ones and the saddest and most difficult. Now think about the length of time those emotions tended to stick around. How did you come down from the highest highs? What brought you up from the lowest lows? These inflection points are useful reminders of the resiliency you have developed over the years. Describe the tools and practices you can use to bounce back from a challenging moment.

2. **Get creative:** Make time to engage in an enjoyable artistic endeavor—photography, drawing, writing, poetry, sculpture, playing an instrument. We all have an inner artist and an inner child who wants to play at creative activities. Artistic activities, when done for pleasure and not perfection, can help you bypass your self-critical mind and downshift from intense emotional highs and lows.

3. **Connect before you direct:** If you are the leader of a project or team initiative, get in the habit of spending a few minutes connecting with your colleagues. Start meetings with an emotional check-in: Ask how people are *feeling* about work, their lives, their projects. This doesn't have to take a lot of time, but it does have to occur regularly on your part so that people come to trust the process.

4. **Get it on paper:** Start a journal. Each evening, spend a few minutes writing down what feelings you experienced that day, using what is called "automatic writing" for five minutes. Take down your emotional highs and lows. It may be just a few words

or a short list. You will be amazed at how just listing your feelings will make you feel better!

Quick-Hit Workout: Beta to Alpha

1. **Only the facts, please:** If you have a tendency to brood—to hang on to feelings of hurt or anger long after the event—consider this daily practice: Spend time each morning or evening journaling about your feelings. Write out your version of the story, and just let the words flow. (No need for beautiful prose!) Get it all down, then ask yourself: "What is 'feeling' here and what is 'fact'?" One of my Wall Street clients got in the habit of writing a quick story of her feelings about work each morning on the commuter train. By the time she reached the office she would end up chuckling at her tendency to wallow in mud of her own making, and she'd walk into the office with renewed vigor.

2. **Get grounded:** Incorporate practices that provide you a sense of serenity: mindful breathing, yoga, meditation, exercise, walks in nature. Spend time with pets or close friends that serve as touchstones, reminding you of what is most important, so you regain perspective.

3. **Tune up, tone down:** List your favorite five acts of self-care—pampering activities that nurture and indulge your body, heart, and mind: sleep, massage, bubble bath, reading fiction, hiking, biking, binge-watching your favorite drama. Enlist a buddy to support you in making sure you do all of them with regularity. The key to leveraging your beta best is balance: Get enough sleep, eat well, and remember to celebrate and honor your emotional states, both high and low.

CHAPTER 7

Be Real:
From Stoic to Vulnerable

Early in my career, as a director of HR at a strategy-consulting firm, I had the opportunity to meet and recruit talented young professionals. In many ways, Jeff was not unusual among the folks I interviewed—smart, exuberant, hardworking—but he was atypical in one respect: Everyone who came into contact with him noticed a gentle sweetness to his personality. Since many of the best and the brightest at places like BCG, McKinsey, and Bain could be a bit competitive and self-centered, wearing their Ivy League ambition on their sleeve, Jeff's combination of traits was rare: friendly, team oriented, and humble.

When he suddenly died just one year later from a brain aneurism at the age of twenty-four, it was shocking. He had just completed a round-the-world tour for a client, conducting analysis of far-flung operations in Asia, India, Africa, and Europe—traveling to more than thirty countries in the space of six weeks. His death was a great loss to all who knew him. The entire team of thirty-plus consultants, including senior leaders and his boss, Dave, made the three-hour trip to the suburbs of Boston for his funeral and burial.

In writing this chapter, I looked back on my career working with hundreds of leaders of all stripes and tried to think of examples of authenticity in action. This brought up the memory of Dave sharing a heartfelt, deeply personal tribute to his young protégé at Jeff's funeral. In the middle of his eulogy, Dave became visibly shaken. Given the circumstances, this might not have been particularly unusual, but here's the thing: No one had ever heard Dave speak with such openness or vulnerability. He was known for being the opposite: tough, analytical, snarky, and acerbic—never soft. In fact, in all the meetings I had attended over the years as his HR rep, I had never even seen him *smile*. He would bark at his staff, and they would scatter to the four corners of the earth to carry out his directives. Even back then, long before Brené Brown had written her bestselling book *Daring Greatly*, about the power of vulnerability, I recognized that this senior consulting partner exhibited more leadership during that eulogy than at any time he fired off a caustic set of instructions at the office. I remember thinking at the time, "Maybe Dave will become a more authentic leader because of Jeff."

I was naïve. Dave was still Dave. This was a funeral, after all, not an ordinary event by any stretch. Dave's demeanor, as real as it had been, did not accompany us back across state lines. I wish I had been his coach at the time to suggest to him: "Keep it up. Stay vulnerable. Be human, let your heart speak more to the troops. You will be a better leader, and our firm will benefit from the full potential of your gifts as you inspire those who follow you, instead of browbeating them into begrudgingly carrying out your orders." But old habits die hard.

It was one of those unforgettable moments when the transient nature of life comes into focus, reminding us how fragile it all is, and how important it is to live to the fullest, with gratitude for every breath. Dave may have returned to his alpha ways, but I was forever changed—both by the loss of Jeff and by the power of seeing through the veil of a hard-nosed leader. Over the many years since, I have coached hundreds of clients with a range of comfort levels with openness and vulnerability to let their hair down, share their deepest values, and speak from the heart. It is only in doing so that we have the power to move all who hear us.

What is your comfort level with being vulnerable in front of others?

Why Be Vulnerable?

Vulnerability starts with the willingness to be honest about what gets in the way of being your most authentic self at work. Is there a specific anxiety or insecurity that holds you back? Are there ways in which you wish you could be more courageous? As a research professor at the University of Houston, Brené Brown conducted hundreds of interviews to discover what lies at the root of social connection, asking, "What does it take to create feelings of belonging?" Her data reveals that the answer is vulnerability.

Vulnerability does not imply weakness or submissiveness. On the contrary, the kind of vulnerability that Brown discovered takes a great deal of courage to express in front of others. The traditional alpha style calls for a leader to be stoic and maintain a distance that minimizes risk, exudes confidence, and limits emotional exposure. This can be a tricky dance for leaders at both ends of the alpha-beta spectrum, because in today's flatter organizations, where young and old work more closely together than ever before, junior staff want to have confidence in their bosses' competence, while at the same time desiring a human connection that brings purpose to their day-to-day. What we might call "position power" holds less sway than in the past. The more the rungs of the ladder get squeezed together, or the ladder is eliminated altogether, the more a leader must engender commitment and loyalty in a different way. Today, vulnerability is strength.

If you come out more alpha on the agility assessment, don't despair. Even alpha leaders have opportunities to show their vulnerable side. Here are just a few you might consider as starting points: check in with an employee who is having a health crisis in her family; reach out to someone who has had a loss; acknowledge that you appreciate assistance with something you find challenging.

What if you find yourself on the wrong side of a conflict? What if you are caught up in an ethical lapse? Consider being open and transparent about a mistake you have made. To err is human, and one of the most empowering ways to rebuild trust is to model your humanity. Depending upon the level of egregiousness involved, consider publicly apologizing and asking for forgiveness. In the cultural upheaval that is occurring in the workplace around sexual harassment and the #metoo movement, being willing to acknowledge transgressions, forthrightly apologize, and demonstrate a willingness to make amends goes a long way toward rehabilitating an individual's integrity in the eyes of others. It takes a strong leader to admit when he has stumbled.

Creating Safe Space

Brené Brown describes vulnerability and authenticity as lying at the root of human connection, which is far too often missing from workplaces. In a leadership development retreat that I regularly conduct for HRC, a human rights advocacy organization, we do an icebreaker where each participant shares one crucial experience from their life journey that led them to become an advocate for others. No one is immune from painful yet pivotal experiences of loss and ill fortune, but everyone's story is different. Some recount moments of discrimination in their work lives, others about challenging family dynamics, but in every case the incident was transformative. We then ask their partner to share the highlights with the larger group as a way of introducing them to the community. The experience is always moving, bringing a sense of shared humanity and trust into the space.[1]

So why is connection and vulnerability so rare in the workplace? We are often taught to keep our distance and project an image of competence and authority. We may share our softer sides with our spouses and friends, but rarely elsewhere, let alone at work. At a corporate retreat, with respect for the more conservative culture of a business environment, I conduct a similar exercise by asking participants to share a "lesson learned along the way" experience. I'm always surprised by how personal they are willing to get if they feel safe and supported by their colleagues. As simple as it sounds, whenever our shared humanity is publicly acknowledged, the connective tissue deepens: After all, we are all on this mysterious journey together.

Research shows that just by looking at someone, we download large amounts of information and can instantaneously register authenticity—or a lack thereof. "We are programmed to observe one another's states so we can more appropriately interact, empathize, or assert our boundaries, whatever the situation may require," says Paula Niedenthal, professor of psychology at the University of Wisconsin–Madison. This process, or "resonance"—how we interpret expressions with speed and nuance—often happens outside of our awareness. In the moment you read someone, you sense their intentions and emotional state, and decide if they can be trusted. Long before we developed language, our ability to interpret signals, both from members of our tribe and strangers, was foundational for creating a sense of community.[2]

Vulnerability and Values: Combustible Cocktail

On a conceptual level, vulnerability as a tool for bringing people closer probably makes sense to you. But let's not underestimate the real disruption that opening up in the workplace can create. Vulnerability is not without risk, so before you take it on, it's important to know what you are getting into. Let's look at a real-life example of how coaching authenticity—vulnerability, transparency, humility—can change a leader and a career. As you read about Sofia, ask yourself: How would you have coached yourself in a similar situation?

The story begins with a call from the senior vice president of HR at a major consumer goods retailer that went something like this: "Hi, Jeff. I wanted to see if you had room in your schedule to coach one of our up-and-coming leaders. Sofia is the head of our global ethics division—a recent addition to the legal department. Overall, she has done a great job, and we are considering bumping her up. Trouble is, Sofia has challenges with her interaction with the other senior team members. She needs to polish her communication style. Sofia is foreign-born and has a rather strong accent. She talks very fast, and gets carried away with dramatic hand gestures and too much detail. She drives the other execs a bit crazy with her long stories. I can't always keep up. We would love for you to help her tone it down and help her become C-suite material."

With that, I was off on an adventure with one of the most talented leaders I have known. Sofia, however, was none too thrilled to hear that she "needed a coach" and was taken aback at the thought that she was viewed as lacking communication skills. That said, she loved her role as the head of an innovative global team responsible for building programs around ethical procurement, wage, and labor practices, all of which were becoming important issues for many large manufacturers. Sofia had the exact job she wanted, with the sort of bully pulpit where she could make a huge difference, so, although she was a bit annoyed about the feedback, she agreed to coaching.

I could see right away what frustrated the executives: Sofia's passion was great, but she did have a habit of speaking very fast, with lots of details and dramatic flourishes, and I struggled at times to follow. At the outset, I thought it was worthwhile to help her become more conscious of her style, to slow down and speak more succinctly.

Six months into the engagement, Sofia was making fantastic progress: She had broken her habit of grand hand gestures (by sitting on her hands) and had learned to practice taking deep breaths before presenting and slowing her cadence to elevate her impact with her audience. It seemed that we were on track for success. But the senior executives consistently failed to notice the changes she made.

The HR executive who had hired me told me, "I can see that she is trying, but she is still too passionate and outspoken. She needs to step back and be more aware of the political dynamics at the top. Not everything on her wish list is possible, not even close. The CEO thinks Sofia needs to be less of a zealot and more of a senior-level businessperson. She needs to get more aligned with the corporate view of her role." I got the idea. Somewhere along the way the expectations for Sofia had clearly taken a turn—and not in her favor. The feedback shifted like sand in the wind, from her needing to be more succinct in her communications to her not having enough "presence" to her being too passionate—even "zealous."

It was especially frustrating, because not only did her peers consider her one of the best leaders in the entire organization, her team loved her so much that many hinted they would leave if she failed to get promoted soon, thus elevating their department to the status it deserved. Her staff told me:

- "We all work as a family because she treats us as such."
- "She knows everyone in the office and has a personal relationship with each one of us."
- "She does not get upset when we make mistakes but gives us the time to learn how to analyze and fix the situation."
- "I always know where I stand with Sofia—she is always open and direct."
- "I trust her because I know her heart is in the right place."

Her peers were equally impressed, if a bit more circumspect about the political dynamic in the office. Many were aware that as a woman with an accent, Sofia would face challenges with the old-school white-male-dominated executive suite. Soon, in fact, that executive suite wound up hiring a Caucasian woman to fill the "newly created" position of global head of sustainability, overseeing social justice, environment, and ethics issues for the entire firm. She was Sofia's new boss. Sofia was shocked and, as you might imagine, incensed. After more than a year of promises about a promotion if she showed more "gravitas," when she did just that, they not only didn't notice, they brought in someone else.

At the end of the day, I think it was Sofia's core strengths—not her accent or communication style—that rankled the top executives: She wore her passion on her sleeve, and she was vulnerable and transparent about how much she cared—about the work, about the company, about the environment and social justice. Vulnerability is absolutely an asset, but it can also be a challenge, for in being open and heartfelt, we expose our most deeply held beliefs. In my coaching with Sofia, it became clear that no matter how diplomatic she was, there was a fundamental disconnect between her principles and the ones held by management. As she told me, "I can modify my communication style, but I can't change my values." To my mind, that is the hallmark of a true leader.

Ultimately, Sofia went on to secure an even bigger role with another global manufacturer where her priorities were in alignment with her bosses'. About a year later, I had the opportunity to hear her present a keynote at a gathering of *Fortune* 100 senior executives on ethical sourcing practices and environmental sustainability. I was blown away by her vision and style—plenty of gravitas. Her growth was remarkable. In a very short time, she had bounced back from her disappointment and hurt, and learned to articulate her ethos in ways that were both efficient and impactful. To me, she represents the loftiest potential of the corporate world, with her values not only intact, but on display. That is the power of vulnerability in action.[3]

Eating Humble Pie

Formerly the director of primary care medicine at a suburban hospital outside Philadelphia, Sarge—a nickname from his military days—was a smart and likable guy. Sarge's boss had demoted him back to a clinical role after receiving complaints from patients and their families about his "arrogance and attitude of disrespect." The CEO of the hospital didn't think it was too late for Sarge to become an effective leader, so I was brought in to help "soften his edges." When the CEO and I met to set up the coaching, I asked, "What could have made a difference for this leader? What could have helped him keep his job?"

He told me that Sarge was hardworking, ethical, efficient, and good at delivering patient care and managing the finances. But then he added, "I need a leader to be in charge, but also to have a softer touch. Sarge is cocky, which, to my mind, is a potentially fatal flaw."

It came down to humility. In today's organizational landscape, humility, like vulnerability, is not a sign of weakness, but an extension of your ability to connect with others, build trust, and express your values. Being "real" presents leaders with a paradox: On the one hand, people value having a sense of certainty that comes from their boss's self-confidence. But younger workers in particular want a sense of connection and even kinship with their coworkers. This balancing act requires a leader to recognize situations in which being humble—which means being aware of blind spots such as arrogance or self-aggrandizement—is crucial to being effective.

My work with Sarge got off to a rocky start. Already humiliated at having been demoted, he was none too thrilled at the idea of having a coach. He spent the bulk of our first meeting complaining about the work environment, his colleagues, and his boss for not backing him up in the face of complaints. "No one really understands how stressful the environment can be," he told me. "You try seeing twenty or thirty patients back-to-back. I admit that I've had a few tough interactions with upset family members, but I always tried to defend my staff and do the right thing. I did lose my cool a few times. Now they want me to go back on the floor without the leadership position and act like nothing ever happened! I wonder if it would be better if I just look for another job."

After letting him vent, I suggested that this demotion could turn out to be the best thing that ever happened to him. He seemed taken aback. "It may sound a bit far-fetched," I admitted, "but for many of the most successful folks out there, those crucible moments of failure and the process of bouncing back and learning from their mistakes transformed them into remarkable leaders."

I shared the story of a similar moment in my own career. I had just taken on my first role as a manager of HR six months earlier. I was sitting across the table from an executive coach who had gathered feedback from my colleagues to share with me. I got some positive feedback, but I was also told that I was "too passionate," and that I needed to "stop being a zealot" and that I was "putting people off by coming across as bossy." I walked out of that room utterly demoralized. It took me weeks to recover, and when I did, I couldn't stop thinking about one line that coach left me with: "Leadership is not always about being in charge. Effective leaders know when to follow and when to lead." I had to learn it the hard way, but it's undergirded my work ever since.

I told Sarge, "It strikes me that there's a real opportunity here. Now that you're back on clinical rounds with your colleagues, you can still be a leader. If you can be a good teammate and foster an environment that brings out the best in everyone, including you, very likely you'll find yourself once again on the short list for a leadership role."

I sent him off to research the power of vulnerability and humility. He returned with a commitment to make three fundamental changes in his style:

- Be transparent and open about personal growth edges.

  Publicly acknowledging his missteps was not easy for Sarge, but he came to see that it was essential. To rebuild trust with colleagues, he needed to be forthright about where he'd gone wrong. The key was to share from a place of authenticity. He decided to express his remorse about any hurtful behavior, to be contrite in response to complaints, and to share how he was committed to growing, both as a leader and a person. It was undoubtedly humbling for him to share his own growth edges with his colleagues, but as he told me later, it had an unexpected effect: His peers, who had previously been wary and kept their distance, started showing up at his office to say how much they admired his honesty and integrity.

- Build personal connections.

    In spending more time with team members, families, and patients, Sarge learned to ask open-ended questions and allow others to vent. It was still true that the ER could get extremely busy and stressful and he often had very limited time for chitchat, but he came to recognize the value of spending those precious few minutes just listening. It was in those moments of openness with his colleagues that he gained useful insights into how best to motivate others, what could be better in the department, and how he could improve the lives of others—all without a specific leadership position.

- Become a good follower.

    At first, Sarge was confused when we discussed that to be a better leader, he would need to know when and how *to follow.* So he sought out highly respected senior physicians who had reputations for what we discussed as "servant leadership." He learned firsthand how the best leaders operate in ways that essentially invert a hierarchy, viewing their roles less about being "the boss" and more as coach and mentor, committed to bringing out the best in others.

A couple of years later, I ran into Sarge in that same hospital. He came running up to announce that he had not only been re-promoted, but was now up for consideration for an administrative role. Obviously, he had come a long way. But what I really noticed was how he talked about the opportunity coming his way: "I'm excited at the possibility of taking on a bigger role. But it doesn't really matter whether I get the job or not. Either way, I'm still leading in all the ways we discussed: leading from below, behind, and across! It would be great to be more formally in charge, but only because I could have even greater impact." His final words were music to my ears: "You know, Jeff, you were right. It did turn out for the best. I guess I needed to be humiliated to become humble."[4]

Too Much of a Good Thing

On the flip side, Cynthia, a software engineer, was offered the opportunity for coaching not because she was too vulnerable or passionate, but because she was "too humble." Having been born and brought up in Korea to respect elders and avoid self-aggrandizement, Cynthia, I assumed at first, had adopted a leadership style that aligned with her culture. But that was an oversimplification. She had attended college in the United States and had already worked here for more than five years when we met.

She had been promoted into supervisory roles based on her engineering skills, garnering respect from colleagues both as an expert and a team player, to the point where she was asked to lead a global training initiative. Her role required extensive travel and managing a team across multiple geographies. She had subordinates and peers from far and wide. She was committed to being viewed as a leader, regardless of her roots.

Much of her managing of others took place over conference calls.

That's where her supervisor noticed that her understated approach might hurt her credibility. It was important for Cynthia to broaden the bandwidth of her communications to ensure that her expertise would be honored, and that colleagues would follow her. She also needed to be willing to be more visible and to showcase her accomplishments. Once she realized that it wasn't necessary to be self-promoting, but that she would gain more traction by projecting confidence and being less hesitant to exert her opinion, she warmed to the idea of coaching.

When she reflected on how she kicked off a training session—she was always up-front, the first to speak—she realized that on the phone she tended to hang back. The difference, it seemed, was that in a classroom, Cynthia could see the faces of her students. Their smiles and enthusiastic body language helped her relax and overcome any anxiety she might feel. That critical element was missing from a conference line. She decided to post a large picture of her team, taken at the kickoff event, over her computer. As simple as it sounds, it worked. With the smiles of her teammates beaming at her, she felt more engaged and comfortable taking the lead—and not just speaking up, but *speaking first*.

The second step was to become more comfortable with recognizing her successes. "I don't want to toot my own horn," Cynthia often told me. "My people deserve the accolades. Don't you think that puffing myself up is unseemly?" Leaving herself out of the equation may have felt honorable, but it diminished how others perceived her value.

I goaded her gently: "If your team of superstars does everything on their own, and you promote their accomplishments while leaving yourself out of the mix, is it possible that the C-suite execs might conclude that your role is unnecessary?" That landed hard, and she admitted that nothing could be further from the truth. The solution was a simple tweak to her language: She could continue to recognize the efforts of her team, but always add an all-important inclusive "we" statement of success: "*We* all pitched in to make the deadline."

Next, we worked on showcasing her accomplishments to key stakeholders. It was especially important for senior management to be aware of her contributions. Even though she was at times mortified by the idea, she understood how her career hinged on it. Cynthia was also committed to being a role model for others on her team, so I prompted her this way: "If you won't showcase your accomplishments for your own advancement, how about keeping in mind the goals of your staff? One of them likely wants a job like yours someday, so you need to prepare them, and yourself, to move on." She got it.

The question then became not whether she would advertise her successes, but how. Here again a bit of self-coaching made all the difference. I asked her to reflect on when and how she had promoted herself in a way that felt comfortable. She told me that throughout her school and professional career she had consciously identified mentors who would "sing her praises" (her words) at the right moment. Here again only a slight behavioral shift was in order. She crafted what I like to call a "stakeholder map"—a framework that identified individuals in her field whom she admired, with whom she had a good rapport, and who would speak highly of her when the time was right. All she had to do was keep them informed of her accomplishments—no need to broadcast or boast publicly.

Ultimately, even a beta leader like Cynthia became more comfortable with the three facets of taking up space: speaking up, speaking first, and being visible. If your natural tendency is also to be more understated, inserting a bit of alpha into your operating mode can be challenging. The pivotal lesson is this: It's not necessary to be less vulnerable or less humble, but rather to stay connected to your values, which means working in an environment that is aligned with them. Keep in mind that humility does not mean being invisible, or minimizing your accomplishments. Effective leadership is not an either-or proposition: You can be humble and visible. You can be modest and accomplished. Most important, you can be vulnerable and strong.

Quick-Hit Workout: Alpha to Beta

1. **Open up:** Look for opportunities to share more about your values, passions, and dreams with your team—subordinates, colleagues, and superiors. You can still retain your privacy; being transparent about your values need not be about your personal life. What matters is that you share from your heart.

2. **Share your edge:** We all have areas for growth. Let your colleagues know what you are working on to develop and improve yourself. As a role model for a growth mind-set, have the courage to declare what you are committed to change. Ask for support. Publicly acknowledge the impact of teachers, coaches, and mentors who helped you get to where you are today.

3. **Own your flaws:** List what you consider your weaknesses and then consider how each "weakness" might be a gift. How has it served you? You'll be surprised about what you will learn. This exercise will help you rewire your brain to accept, with a bit of levity, those aspects of yourself that you would prefer to ignore or wish away.

4. **Thank your failures:** Be proud of your failures. Be willing to acknowledge mistakes made along your path. In a journal, list

the "low points" or moments of disappointment and ask yourself, "What did I learn from this so-called failure? How did it help me grow?"

Quick-Hit Workout: Beta to Alpha

1. **Speak first:** Find a buddy or colleague who you trust and ask them to be your coach—reminding you not just to speak up, but to *speak first* as appropriate. Place a touchstone somewhere you'll see regularly (printed out and hung over your desk, or used as your phone's wallpaper or computer screensaver), which will prompt you to engage when your instinct is to hold back.

2. **Showcase—not show off—your gifts:** Regularly update your résumé and social media to highlight your strengths and accomplishments on platforms such as LinkedIn. Look at profiles of colleagues you admire, and emulate them; reach out and ask for references from people who you know will sing your praises.

3. **"We" the people:** When you make a point of recognizing others, be sure to include yourself in the mix. Write "I, We, You" in a place that you will see regularly, and get a buddy to monitor your inclusive language.

4. **Seize the day:** Look for opportunities to teach or mentor others, where you can comfortably take the step into a position of power.

Anyone Can Lead

In the spring of 2016, I received an invitation to partner with my good friend and colleague Leslie to design and facilitate a leadership development program for people with disabilities. The first of its kind in the United States, the program was initiated by the city of Chicago to celebrate the twenty-fifth anniversary of the Americans with Disabilities Act. The twenty participants had been through a rigorous selection process, were all working or aspiring to work in leadership roles in their chosen professions, and although they had a range of disabilities, they all had one crucial attribute in common: None of them viewed their disability as an impediment to becoming a leader. Any preconceived notion that I may have held was quickly wiped away as I witnessed each person show up fully, not merely *overcoming* any impediment, but integrating it as a stepping-stone to success.

As we explored themes that may now sound familiar to you— leadership styles, emotional intelligence, giving and receiving feedback, collaboration—I witnessed over and over what I had always believed: True leadership emanates from within. Every participant was simply fierce: committed to showing up, being vulnerable, asking for help, and practicing new skills with confidence and humor. Imagine being asked to "listen deeply" when you are deaf; to "walk the walk" when you use a wheelchair; to focus on "blind spots" when you are blind. Leslie and I became deeply and humbly aware of how biased our language can be, and how our perceptions of what it means to be "disabled" are mostly misperceptions.

In the years since this program, Chicago has continued its commitment to leadership training for people with disabilities. Similar programs are expanding to New York City, Los Angeles, and beyond. My own experience confirmed what I had long preached: With a dose of vulnerability, humility, and a willingness to grow, we are all natural leaders.

PART III

Somatic Leadership

CHAPTER 8

You Are More Than a Brain on a Stick

Remember Mark, the surgeon who exemplified flexibility in action? I went into our interaction thinking that surely the mental training and discipline needed to be a surgeon would put him squarely into the cerebral "thinker" category. But what I saw on the ground upended my expectations, as it often does. Mark was always on the move, his work equal parts brain and brawn, and even his emotions manifested physically: He leaned into his audience, reached out, hugged and touched people. He was a mover, a shaker, a shape-shifter. A somatic leader.

No matter how cerebral or emotive you are at baseline, who you are as a leader shows up in your speaking, thinking, acting, and physical expression. At some level, we are all somatic creatures—everything we think, feel, and do emerges from within the bodies in which we live. We have for too long focused leadership training almost exclusively from the neck up. What we overlook is the immense value of being able to accurately read and respond to our sensory experience of the world.[1]

Somatic intelligence is the ultimate purveyor of those gut feelings that we may publicly dismiss, preferring to bolster our arguments with reams of data—but we always come back to it in a crisis. As we delve into the mechanics of collaboration and engagement, be on the lookout for ways to, as Buddhist monk and teacher Taisen Deshimaru would say, "think with your whole body."[2]

When you stop and reflect on your own physical presence, it may surprise you to realize how much time you spend off-balance, approaching colleagues with closed arms, gazing at the floor or ceiling, or avoiding eye contact. The effects are subtle. But how we show up in our bodies at any given moment is one of the most powerful indicators of where we stand, of who we are—and it is what others "read" before anything else. In my leadership workshops, when we discuss somatic awareness, I ask the participants to reflect and practice modeling four physical attributes, as noted below.

Take a moment and reflect on the chart. Give yourself a number from 1 (for each opportunity area) to 5 (for each strength; something you do naturally) in these four domains:

Open	☐ 1	☐ 2	☐ 3	☐ 4	☐ 5
Centered	☐ 1	☐ 2	☐ 3	☐ 4	☐ 5
Grounded	☐ 1	☐ 2	☐ 3	☐ 4	☐ 5
Flexible	☐ 1	☐ 2	☐ 3	☐ 4	☐ 5

As with all of the assessments in this book, there is no right or wrong. This is an opportunity to think about and coach yourself, to stretch beyond customary patterns. As you read this chapter, keep coming back to this chart. Ask yourself: "How do I exhibit *openness* with my body? Where do I shut down?" "What does it feel like—and look like—to be *centered* in mind and body? What knocks me off-center?" "How do I *ground* myself and stay grounded, even if the world around me is a swirl of activity?" "What does it mean to demonstrate *flexibility,* not just as a leader but, specifically, in my body?"

Leadership is much more than a cerebral or even emotional endeavor. Let's dive in to the four main areas of research that prove it: body as language, the science of intuition, the leadership dojo, and the environment.

Body as Language

The body can be your greatest support, or undermine you. Multiple studies have shown that paying attention to your physical stance, taking time to ground and align your body, especially in times of stress or anxiety (for example, before an important presentation), can reinvigorate your sense of confidence and competence—positioning you, literally and figuratively, for success.

Are you aware of how your body speaks? The place to start understanding the science of somatic leadership is with your own body—how it supports or detracts from the message you want to send. Just as with emotional intelligence, a key component of non-verbal communication is the direct and indirect ways in which our physical behavior transmits instant signals to those around us. Your emotional state, whatever it is, is communicated so quickly that any misalignment between what you say and how you present is immediately evident. The body speaks much louder, and much faster, than words. Effective somatic leadership, whether you're naturally inclined toward the kinesthetic or more cerebral and/or emotional, means gaining awareness of how your nonverbal communication aligns—or not—with your words.

At first blush, I thought Joshua simply had a nervous tic. This was his first time working with a coach, so perhaps he was intimidated. Highly ambitious, fast moving, and intellectually robust, at the ripe old age of thirty-two he had taken a leap from his corporate job in marketing to found a tech business. The company had quickly grown from the original founders and a handful of contractors to a team of more than two hundred, developing apps for smartphones in the e-commerce space. Joshua was enthusiastic about hiring a coach for his CFO, his new head of sales, and other members of the expanding team, and he recognized the positive message it would send if he also submitted to coaching.

My first introduction to the organization took place at a town hall. Joshua spoke eloquently and passionately about the goals of the company, the pace of growth, and his desire to build a high-powered, motivated team. He had the basics of executive presentation down: He was not overly stiff or formal, gestured at appropriated times, spoke engagingly, and, most important, focused his entire body on the audience. This company was clearly his dream come true, and his ability to communicate that fueled his team's desire to succeed. I came away impressed.

Later that day, however, when we had our first one-on-one, I could barely believe I was across the table from the same person who had whipped his colleagues into a frenzy of excitement. Joshua was stiff, blunt, and distracted, and his body language—fidgeting, vibrating, shaking—sent unmistakable signals that he wanted to be anywhere else but there. Below the neck, he was anything but calm. He still spoke fairly confidently, though, so I wrote it off as jitters.

Trouble is, three sessions later I still found myself distracted by the obvious discomfort emanating from Joshua, which came through in everything except his speaking. Our physical presence is vital to how we impact others, but there's no right or wrong way to show up so long as your physical presence and your words match up. With Joshua, there was an obvious disconnect. His speech was clear, authoritative, and succinct, with a cadence and tone that was classic alpha. But his body was telling another story.

I took a deep breath, leaned in, put my palms calmly on the table, and asked, with as little judgment as I could manage, "Are you aware that your legs are vibrating under the table? Are you aware that you're constantly fidgeting with either your phone or your pen or whatever's handy?"

He looked stunned. "Yeah," he replied, face reddening. "I just have a lot of extra energy. I find it difficult to focus in one-on-one meetings because I'm constantly thinking about what I need to get done."

I told him, "Well, the to-do list may be in the back of your mind, but it's playing out front and center—on your fingers, in your legs and feet. The reason I bring it up today is because I realized that it is making *me* nervous."

"Wow," Joshua said. "It never dawned on me that my nervous energy might have a negative impact on you."

I told him that it would be important—not just for my nerves, but for his success as a leader—to match his mannerisms with his speaking pattern and demeanor. Otherwise, his team might feel that he was difficult to read, even untrustworthy. In our next session, he was a bit calmer but still fidgeting, and he brought tons of questions about presence. We were soon exploring ways that he could break himself of these nervous habits.

The trick to developing new habits begins with a desire to change. Joshua would never modify his behavior just because I told him to, at least not permanently; he had to *want* to show up differently, and then design practices that he could track, reinforce, and celebrate. First, he investigated the source of his anxiety. He confided that he did worry about the future of the organization, despite his confident demeanor in front of a group. He sometimes felt he was in over his head, overwhelmed by his responsibility for his employees. I told him that every entrepreneur I had ever worked with had nightmares about failure; it came with the territory, and was nothing to be ashamed of or to hide.

We explored how he could become more comfortable expressing vulnerability and transparency with his team (which he initially had thought was a very bad idea). As I said to him, "Though it's not in front of the whole group, your anxiety is palpable in a small group or one-on-one, so why not be honest about it? My prediction is that your team will respect you more, not less."

This idea of revealing his true feelings didn't go down easy, but Joshua agreed to take a tiny step, starting with a few colleagues that he trusted. Of course, they already knew that Joshua was anxious—they could intuit the signals as well as me—so not only did they receive his revelations graciously, they told me later that they were relieved, and impressed, that he was becoming, as they put it, "more human." The blessing of vulnerability is that it connects us all to our deeper humanity. It worked for Joshua.

The second path we followed was more practical. Joshua needed to calm his body in sit-down situations. But how could he break his twitching habit if it happened unconsciously most of the time? I suggested that, much like breaking a smoking habit or any other ingrained behavior that gives us a momentary reprieve from stress, he would need practices that would provide some relief, while being less of a distraction. He agreed to put his cellphone out of reach during meetings, and he asked his colleagues to do the same. It wasn't an easy ask of himself or others, but with the goal for greater focus and attention, he took up the challenge.

Secondly, he found a touchstone—an object to help ground his energy whenever he felt the tics coming on (not a rubber band or a pen that would reinforce the constant motion). It turned out to be a beautiful fist-size piece of stone cut with weathered blue sea glass. Holding the stone had a calming effect on Joshua, and when people asked about it, he could share the story of the beach where he found it—a small diversion that was endearing and relaxing for everyone. Finally, for his restless leg, a habit he had picked up way back in grammar school, I suggested he consider moving around more often, as it seemed to discharge his energy in a less distracting manner. There was no reason why he couldn't talk standing up, leaning against a window, or walking with a colleague.

Success for Joshua came down to awareness of a simple fact: His body was speaking for him whether he liked it or not. His challenge—as is true for all of us—was to align the words, tone, and pace of his speaking with his physical presence. With newfound self-awareness and practices he could rely upon, Joshua was soon sitting calmly, sometimes holding his touchstone, sometimes not, able to make a conscious decision about how to be in each moment.[3]

The Silenced Woman

When I first met Linda, a senior vice president of research at a major biopharmaceutical company, her leadership style was more beta than alpha, consensus oriented, inquisitive, and unassuming—but she was super driven and had lofty goals and high expectations of herself. She was matter-of-fact, even unemotional and dry, as you might expect from someone steeped in science—a quintessential cerebral leader.

But she was experiencing conflict with a new boss, who had a more alpha, authoritarian style. As Linda's upward trajectory now seemed derailed, she was feeling marginalized. Her question for me: "My new boss denigrates me in front of colleagues, does not invite me to key meetings with senior people, and relegates me to low-level administrative work. I think she sees me as a threat, just because I'm smart and hardworking. What should I do?"

Not only that, some of her less experienced male colleagues were being promoted. She felt demoralized and unmotivated. Our work for the first few months was by phone, and even though I could tell from her tone that her work atmosphere was less than ideal, it wasn't until we met in person that I realized how her physical presence was reinforcing the negative dynamic. Over lunch, her story still sounded familiar, but something was different from our phone sessions. By the time dessert arrived, it was evident: Her tendency to look down at the floor, furrow her brow, scowl, cross her arms, and slouch all were uncannily incongruous with her way of speaking.

Linda's emotional state was making itself known, no matter how much she tried to cover with powerful words. I suggested that she work on standing tall, holding her head high, unlocking her arms, putting her shoulders back, facing forward, and making direct eye contact. She would also project more self-confidence if she took deep breaths and shook her jaw, shoulders, and arms loose on a regular basis, especially when she had to interact with her condescending boss.

As we continued to work together, Linda opened up to me about the physical symptoms that had been taking a toll on her for some time, at least since her tough and condescending boss had entered the scene: insomnia, depression, and migraine headaches, just to name a few. As she came to recognize, the body must not be ignored. We explored times in her life when she had felt strong. In her teenage years, she had been a competitive horseback rider. Her teenage daughter was currently a championship dressage rider, and she could see her confident younger self reincarnate. The somatic dance between horse and rider became a model for the kind of embodied power that Linda had lost touch with.

Linda's story is an example of what emerging research indicates is a form of post-traumatic stress syndrome that is occurring across the leadership landscape, as women and people of color rise to senior roles in organizations that have heretofore been exclusively a white men's club. In a research project sponsored by the Institute of Coaching, executive coach and organization consultant Carrie Arnold interviewed more than fifty women who have felt silenced and traumatized by our patriarchal culture that far too often still shuts down women who choose to lead. Arnold concluded that the act of being dismissed, condescended to, or just ignored, can have emotional and even physical ramifications, like with Linda. For many of the women Arnold studied, illnesses such as fibromyalgia, irritable bowel syndrome, and chronic fatigue syndrome were common, along with severe back pain, depression, and insomnia.[4]

Moreover, Carrie's research indicates that the perpetrators of this trauma are not always men. The diminishment of women's voices may have originated in the boys' club of the executive suite, but its legacy lives on. As leaders and coaches, we must watch closely for symptoms with our female clients—manifestations of that oppression that may show up first in the body, as pain, illness, depression, or issues with burnout, sleep, sugar, and food. It is crucial that we all be on the lookout for the suffering caused by silencing, and take steps to help our clients—and ourselves—reclaim their physical power.

Intuition and the Space Between

It started out as team building; it ended up a revelation. My partner Pascal and I were asked by our client, the VP of financial products at a major European bank, to lead a half-day session for thirty sales and marketing professionals in the middle of their three-day off-site meeting in Lisbon. The idea was to get the group out of the hotel and create an experience where they would have an opportunity to learn, not only about one another but about the city, the culture, and the people. None of them spoke Portuguese.

We devised a scavenger hunt and sent them into the city. They had two hours to collect subway tokens, local newspapers, packaged local foods, menus, and so on. In the search, the teams would have to interact with the locals, convincing them to share information or stuff from their workplace. Back at the conference center, they would use those objects to build a sculpture that symbolized their adventure and new knowledge.

Our goal was for the employees to mix it up, break down silos, get to know one another better, take a bit of risk. What we hadn't expected was how these cerebral banker types would find innovative ways to engage with the locals, overcoming linguistic and cultural distance, as well as any anxiety they may have had about traversing an unknown landscape. The objects they found, the way they creatively combined them, and the stories they shared about connecting with strangers not only resulted in spectacular sculptures, but translated into a deep conversation about the power of reaching out, breaking down barriers, and, most important, following intuition.

In the years since, I've created many versions of this initiative to help different teams get out of their heads and into their bodies, to get out in the world, to make intuitive leaps, create connections, and investigate new ways of seeing and being in the world. Researchers agree that creativity and intuition are inextricably connected to the body. Somatic leadership requires a willingness to respect and integrate *intuition* into your day-to-day. No matter how much value you may place on data or analytics, in the end, breakthroughs come from taking leaps beyond what the data tells you and seeing through walls that exist only in your mind.[5]

The Leadership Dojo

My dear friend Tom Lutes is a black belt aikido master and leadership trainer, at whose seminars I always deepen my insight into the connection between mind and body. His work is all about enhancing our ability to interpret and respond effectively to the movements and countermovements of others—just the kind of thing a leader needs to do in today's volatile world.

The basic philosophy of aikido developed in the early twentieth century as an extension of the Japanese martial art jujitsu. The practice consists of body postures and movements that enable a "warrior" to neutralize an opponent and respond to an unplanned attack. In one of the moves Tom teaches, opponents start in opposite corners of the dojo ("space for learning" in Japanese), looking at each other with intention. They meet in the center, make a 360-degree turn, and sweep toward the opposite corner. The goal is to "meet" your opponent without touching, to come as close as possible while remaining energetically engaged with direct eye contact, arriving in the exact position where your opponent stood just moments before. It sounds easy, but in this graceful dance, each participant must develop their balance; otherwise they may end up off-kilter, bump into each other, and twirl out of control.

Lutes is a student and partner of Richard Strozzi-Heckler, the author of *The Art of Somatic Coaching*, who founded an institute to apply the principles of aikido to the art and skill of leadership. Over thirty years ago, Strozzi was invited to bring his training to the U.S. Marine Corps. Strozzi found that even though the soldiers were focused and strong, they lacked the necessary resilience and adaptability to respond well to the unpredictable dynamics of modern warfare. Aikido, Strozzi believed, could substantially augment their preparedness by integrating mind, body, and spirit. It could also be effectively applied to leadership in all situations. Since then, he's trained a wide variety of leaders, from start-up entrepreneurs to *Fortune* 500 CEOs, and researchers have demonstrated the benefits of martial arts traditions that integrate intellectual, emotional, and somatic intelligence.[6]

What was powerful about learning a basic aikido move was that it gave us an opportunity to experience a dynamic that imitates real life. Think about it: Every time you walk down a crowded sidewalk and encounter a stranger, there is a fleeting decision to make: Do you step aside? Do you hold your ground and make the stranger move around you? Human interactions regularly involve a similar dance of power. Aikido reenacts how, in today's less hierarchical configurations, effective leaders toggle back and forth between the energies of power *over* others and power *with* others. The best leaders exert power and direct when needed, but are also quick to shift into a receptive, responsive mode that encourages the full expression of their colleagues and peers: They can move from alpha to beta and back.

The Corporate Dojo

"I'm frustrated, Jeff," Bob exclaimed. "They want me to do so much, but the CEO refuses to give me direct line authority over the business line execs." Bob was feeling derailed and caught off guard when, less than one year after he joined his financial software products firm as chief operating officer, he was asked by the CEO to integrate functions from three different divisions. Even though the CEO had indicated that Bob would have "direct line authority" for the purposes of this initiative, it was also clear that since he was the new kid on the block, those words rang hollow. The three general managers had all been running their own product lines for many years with a great deal of autonomy, and despite varying levels of success, it was a stretch to believe they would acquiesce to his authority, no matter what the CEO said.

When I first started coaching Bob, he struck me as obsessed over his box on the organization chart and was feeling set up for failure. He assumed, as many leaders do, that to be successful, he would need to have direct authority over the business line execs. But, as I explained, as organizations become flatter, that traditional type of authority is less and less critical to a leader's clout and advancement.

"I get that I need to use what you call 'influence power' rather than direct control," he replied, "but how do I go about doing it?" Bob's style was beta—consensus building, democratic, diplomatic—so we began to talk about how to best influence his three colleagues, all of whom were more alpha, if they refused to report to him. Initially, he wanted to go to the CEO and complain, but instead we brainstormed about how to reframe his dilemma to see it as an opportunity to exert his leadership in more creative ways.

As an avid athlete, he was intrigued when I suggested that the philosophy of aikido might be useful as he convinced his colleagues to work with him. Specifically, we discussed stance (*kamae*), adaptability (*tai sabaki*), and freestyle (*randori*). The first principle, *kamae* in Japanese, focuses on paying close attention to the physical, mental, and emotional ground with which he approached his colleagues. Bob would need to take stock of how he showed up and develop practices to stay centered—to not be reactive or show his frustration—if they resisted his requests. Key to success would be to not take their words or actions personally, to retain his balance in the face of an "attack."

One of his colleagues, a woman who had been running her division with total autonomy for many years, could be dismissive, verging on rude, if she disagreed with someone. Bob, who was African American, was sensitive to not being perceived as a stereotypical "angry black man," so we discussed how best to hold his ground. We also discussed the fear-based triggers that might be surfacing for her: Loss of autonomy? Lack of control? Uncertainty about her future? Bob's goals were clear: to hold his stance, breathe, remain calm, and instead of responding with a counterattack, to do the opposite in good aikido praxis and exhibit empathy. By meeting her anger with kindness, he could render her attack inert.

The second theme, *tai sabaki*, meant taking a different approach to his colleagues, one where he focused proactively, not just on his own objectives, but on their needs, seeing them not so much as opponents but partners. In real-world terms, this involved crafting win-win scenarios he could share whenever he sensed that a request might be met with resistance. For example, when he knew that they would resist giving up control over some functions—as his initiative called for consolidation and cost savings—he was up-front with how the shared savings would benefit not just the firm, but each of them personally in the form of increased bonuses.

Finally, in *randori*, the aikido practitioner must hold her ground in the face of multiple attackers. The idea was for Bob to stay centered in case of any attempt, from any direction, to derail him. This meant preparing for resistance, not just from the senior executives but also from underlings or from other parts of the organization that were politically motivated to undermine his efforts. *Randori* is akin to walking through Grand Central at rush hour. How do you move through the crowd? Do you step aside and let others pass? Will you get to your destination if you always play polite? Or do you plow ahead (in true New Yorker style) and send an indisputable signal: Get out of my way!

Bob's success came down to applying a reflective approach to how he interacted with his colleagues—to be directive at times, but also receptive and diplomatic—seeking a win-win wherever possible. Many of my clients now work in matrixed configurations where the power relationships are less than straightforward. Authority and control are constantly shifting. Just as the world is becoming more and more chaotic, so are the internal dynamics of organizations. *Randori* teaches us to stay centered and be flexible in situations in flux—a perfect metaphor for today's leadership. Bob not only succeeded in integrating redundant functions of the three business lines, saving the firm thousands of dollars, he reached a new level of partnership with those tough-guy executives, whom he initially viewed as foes.

The Environment

When Tim asked me if I'd be interested in facilitating an off-site meeting with his leadership team in Hawaii, in January, I jumped at the chance. A paid vacation, right? Well, yes and no. While it is true that Hawaii is a sweet getaway for anyone based in Boston in the middle of winter, it was a lot of hard work, both for me and the team, with contentious meetings that on occasion lasted from early morning until long after sunset. Of course, with breaks for hiking, golf, and swimming, it also turned out to be a great locale for the team to connect, let their hair down, and get to know one another.

It may seem intuitive that a team meeting on a beach in Polynesia is likely to go better than one held on the thirtieth floor of an office tower in Massachusetts. The deeper truth is that the strategic planning under discussion by this group of physician leaders would have been challenging and combative in any setting. They needed to make decisions about policies and investments that would impact the organization for years to come and, at least at first, not everyone was aligned. As the board chair, Tim knew they needed a facilitator so that he could engage with the team as a colleague and peer, able to contribute without having to direct the conversation.

He also understood the value of being in an environment conducive to disconnecting from the day-to-day distractions of the work itself. Not only was I able to facilitate and, as an outsider, bear the brunt of some of the intense energy from participants who had strong feelings one way or another, but they could also break from their conversations and go hiking, swim, play golf, and generally connect. What really made the event a success was Tim's awareness of the need for both work and play and the benefits of integrating social activities and exercise into the dynamic.

Location matters. Atmosphere matters. Many of my clients are coming to understand this, even the ones without the financial wherewithal to whisk their top executives off to a tropical island. More and more leaders are understanding how the environment impacts the creativity, the energy, and the performance of their teams. The research consistently points to the value of paying attention to the landscape, the atmosphere, the balance of private versus communal space, and the connection (or disconnection) from nature. For humans to live up to their full potential, we need to think beyond our physical bodies into the spaces, virtual and literal, where we hang our hats, work, and play. Our space is an extension of our being.[7]

The natural world is our greatest teacher, whether it's a hundred-year-old willow in Central Park or a flowing river on the edge of a small town in Oregon. When we take ourselves outside and interact with nature, we reconnect with a visceral truth: One fundamental source of all of our creative energy is the earth itself. My creativity coach, Jennifer Wilhoit, author of *Writing on the Landscape,* reminds me that whenever she feels stuck in her writing or on a creative project, she takes a walk in the woods, gets down on her hands and knees, and touches the earth. "Beauty begets beauty," she says. "Nature is always available to us, to center and remind us of its bounty. To replenish our energy, reinvigorate our sense of wonder, we need to stop, look, touch, and connect to the ultimate source, the place where all the energy of creativity is born: Mother Earth."[8]

A walking meditation doesn't just mean taking in the view, even though that may be a nice shift from the office. Feeling the earth under your feet, touching the stones you see, holding a fallen leaf in your hand—these simple acts can calm and center you. The simple act of bearing witness to the beauty of the world moves our energy away from self-concern, endless to-do lists, and frustrations with the creative process, reminding us that we live in a much grander landscape than the gray zone bounded by our ears.

If you feel a creative or interpersonal block, walk through woods, beach, field, or stream, or make a point of watching the sunrise or sunset. Your spark will reignite, for beauty begets beauty: What is out there is in you, too. It is available to all of us, always. As we move into leadership practices that combine individuals into creative, high-performing teams, note that the latest science emphasizes the importance of breaking down man-made siloes between head, heart, and gut. Every new idea that comes into this world, whether scientific breakthrough or world-class art, begins its journey in a complex web of neurotransmitters, biochemical secretions, muscles, neurons, and synapses. For all our rational prowess, we never transcend the body, and the body never transcends the earth. From head to toe, our bodies are finely tuned instruments of nature, of connection, and of creation itself.

CHAPTER 9

Be Collaborative:
From Power to Partnership

As we move into chapters on collaboration and engagement, stop and ask yourself, What makes for world-class collaboration? Do you know any superb collaborators? What do they do? When I pose these questions, the first thing my clients say is that great collaborators are great listeners. Absolutely, right on! And how do great listeners listen? By creating safe space for others to speak, taking time to attend to what is said, making sure everyone is understood—and by showing respect through their words, gestures, and *physical attentiveness*. We are now in 3-D territory. What I mean by that is this: Well-baked collaboration makes a delicious three-layer (cognitive, emotional, somatic) leadership cake—a recipe that brings out the best in all.

When I first met Paula, she struck me as gregarious and friendly, with a creative spark that made me like her right away. I found it hard to imagine that anyone would find it difficult to work with her. She didn't initially come across as authoritative or bossy, let alone harsh or abusive. Still, my intuition told me that, at heart, Paula was not so much a strong alpha dog as someone who had reached the zenith of her options in managing a team and was falling back on being bossy. She described her leadership style as flexible and collaborative, but she also acknowledged that she had high expectations of herself and her team. She made some big, even grandiose, claims, such as, "I come up with great ideas and present winning strategies" for the firm's clients. But she wasn't far off the mark: Just four years into her career as a project lead for digital media, she had proven herself capable with her presentation skills, ideas, and willingness to try out approaches that not only impressed her superiors, but kept the clients coming back for more. Her boss told me she was a talent to watch.

But I had been told in confidence by this very same boss that her team was burning out, and she was churning through staff. A few junior associates even refused to work with her. It was awkward to get her to consider that she might not have the collaborative reputation that she thought. Feedback, as we have discussed, is especially important—and difficult—for overachievers. Early on, Paula admitted that she sometimes struggled with the complexity of the company's matrixed organizational structure. As a creative director, she recruited graphic artists, designers, software engineers, and analytics staff—all of whom typically had a reporting relationship to someone else—to work on her projects. It was a challenge to get people working in sync since she did not have direct authority over them. She told me, "If I could only hire my own people and train them up, we'd win even more business."

Her unwillingness to accept any accountability for her team's dynamic made it clear: She was impressive, yes, but had critical blind spots. As with most of my millennial clients, Paula was incredibly well-intentioned: She believed in coaching, valued feedback (especially when it was positive), and was committed to creating a balanced work experience for herself and her team. I had seen it before. By all appearances, she should have been set up for career glory. But in today's nonhierarchical workplaces, effective collaboration is probably the single biggest challenge that young leaders must tackle. They face a dual challenge: Workers want feedback, support, and direction—but not a traditional alpha boss. I asked Paula to focus on two questions: How do you lead a group of people over whom you don't have a lot of direct control and who may be focused on their own career growth? What if those same employees are willing to work hard, but only in a collegial atmosphere?

Paula had succeeded rapidly at winning contracts, impressing clients, and building a reputation at the firm for being innovative and hardworking, but by the time I met her, that reputation was double-edged: The senior execs thought of her as a rising star, while her peers and junior staff saw her as self-centered and enamored of her own contribution. She rarely involved her team in client presentations, tended to stifle dissenting voices, and never hesitated to take the credit with a client. Paula would either be vaulted to the top or on her way out the door. Luckily, she realized she had reached that threshold and was willing to reflect on how her strengths could be complemented with greater self-awareness and collaborative skills. She told me she wanted to get it right.

Paula conquered the essential challenge of leadership today: collaboration that works. There is no magic formula, but there are many evidence-based stages that every effective leader must navigate successfully:

1. Optimize your use of power.

2. Assess and nurture talent.

3. Turn a disparate group into an aligned team.

4. Provide useful—and usable—feedback.

5. Foster a safe environment.

6. Empower with mentoring and coaching.

The goal is to create a culture of collaboration, where employees not only become loyal to their boss and their company (not an easy feat in today's mercurial business climate), but thrive.

The Exercise of Power

Many of my coaching engagements start with a discussion of power. An awareness of how one gets and uses it—from the stage, across the table, on the phone, or over video—is fundamental to everything that comes later. "Being collaborative" is easy to say but difficult to accomplish if you are unaware of how, where, and why you exert influence. Leadership is all about the use of that power—but it must be a conscious, conscientious use. Whenever we exert power, no matter how delicately, with little awareness of our natural strengths and tendencies, how can we hope to expand our repertoire?

Paula agreed that exerting influence in an inspiring way would be key to her success. But when I asked her what kinds of power she used, she could come up with only the obvious varieties: positional power and expert power. When I suggested there are as many as ten types of power she could access, she was surprised.

Here's the list that I shared with Paula. Reflect on the types of power you use. Power is energy exerted from one object onto another. What matters is how it is applied.

1. **Positional power:** Comes from organizational authority or position (the starting point for Paula as a "director")—often forgotten by people with the power; rarely forgotten by those without it.

2. **Referred power:** Comes from an external source—delegated or given credence based on the credibility and connections of others (for example, a peer who is respected by senior management augments your own power).

3. **Expert power:** Comes from wisdom, experience, and skills (someone is widely respected because of their knowledge of social media).

4. **Ideological power:** Comes from an idea, vision, or analysis. It can be an original thought or brainstorm, an ideal such as "self-love" or "liberation," or a historically based ideology, such as democracy or capitalism.

5. **Obstructive power:** Stems from the ability to coerce, block, or resist, whether implicitly or explicitly. It can increase leverage of other forms. Many activists are experts in its use.

6. **Personal power:** Personal energy, persuasive skills, emotional resonance, contagious enthusiasm, magnetism, charisma.

7. **Institutional power:** Economic, legal, and political power directly wielded by positions associated with institutions (it may come with "membership" privilege, clearance, and the like).

8. **Cultural power:** The expression of cultural norms, conditioning, and privilege regarding race/class/gender identification. Like positional power, it is often underpinned with economic and educational privilege or superiority.

9. **Network power:** The extension of influence through a non-hierarchical web or matrix of connections to spread a message outward, engaging and spurring action in others ("the ripple effect").

10. **Peer power or co-powering:** Activated when leaders exert power in reciprocal ways that enhance the status of both parties, leveraging the personal power of *others* through modeling, validating, and feedback.[1]

Once I laid it out, Paula not only recognized most of the other forms of power, but she regularly used them with her team. She understood immediately that she was employing not only positional and expert power, but referred power—for example, whenever she leveraged the knowledge and connections she had with others. She chuckled when I asked her for examples of how she employed obstructionist power, recounting the times she had stood up in the face of resistance from other senior leaders or even from a client. She knew she had a reputation for not backing down, and most of the time that had worked in her favor—but when I noted that she seemed to have applied obstructionist power with her own staff, she was aghast.

"It was never intentional," she admitted. "Sometimes I do put my foot down and demand action, but I don't see myself as threatening or dogmatic."

"Really?" I pushed a bit. "Are you aware of how your strong directives may land on junior staff?"

"Well, it is true that I always try to soften the message when it comes to clients, but I have less patience and higher expectations with my team."

"Power dynamics in action," I noted.

"I get it," she replied. "I need to be more cognizant of what power I have and how I use it."

Paula understood the importance of partnering with others and expanding her connections, and she knew that these were underleveraged arrows in her power quiver. Many millennials like her are more motivated by peer-to-peer influences than by displays of force, so we discussed that she might leverage her team more effectively if she worked on her network power. She was a bit confounded by this, since her primary focus was on clients. She had always thought that building relationships within her network would take a lot of time, and she felt pressure to get results quickly.

This is a common complaint. Many of my more alpha clients logically know the value of co-powering, but they perceive demands from senior management and clients as higher priority. I reminded her that every great leader wakes up at some point to an obvious truth: Focusing on employee satisfaction is just as important, because without them there would be no clients. I suggested that just spending fifteen minutes engaging with key associates on her project teams or in other parts of the firm, or asking her staff to cooperate more actively, would *not* set her back but might actually save time. As an extra benefit, she would potentially shift her reputation from being an "all roads lead to me"–type boss.

When I asked Paula to reflect on some of the most valuable

moments in her own career trajectory, she acknowledged that what had catapulted her upward were the conversations she'd had with the people who came before her or above her—her mentors. She appreciated how much having feedback and attention to her personal goals had mattered, especially in a work landscape that could be difficult to navigate, with few direct paths. Networking, leveraging peer relationships, and building coalitions both inside and outside her line of authority had been, and would continue to be, essential to her success.[2]

The necessary mind shift came down to recognizing that she needed her colleagues if she was going to succeed. Because of the demands of the environment, and her action-oriented and decisive style, it wasn't likely that Paula would ever become a beta leader, but that was fine. What did change was her awareness of the importance of being more inclusive and a better listener, and inviting her colleagues to an occasional coffee—leveraging, valuing, and validating the contribution of others.

Up Periscope

The next step is optimizing the talents of each member of any group you lead. Build from the bottom up—from strength to strength. The understandable mistake that managers in matrixed environments tend to make is that when they recruit individuals from other teams for a short-term project, they home in exclusively on the competency needed to accomplish that task. This makes sense, but it also creates a situation in which the individual has been co-opted solely for their piece of the puzzle and is then expected to return to their core group. I asked Paula to put herself in the place of a functional expert or junior staff member getting pulled into a project and then dismissed. How would that feel?

"I see the risk," she admitted. "Even though their direct manager is technically responsible for their career growth, I know that if it were me I would come away feeling used."

The key to success is to not see team members as cogs in your project machine, but to view them more broadly—yes, as resources for your current needs, but also for the strategic growth of the firm. Try shifting your perspective upward, viewing the landscape with a wide-angle lens. If you raise the periscope, so to speak, projecting yourself in the future to a more significant leadership role, then you begin to view the people that join you, even if temporarily, as part and parcel of the company's overall capabilities. Their personal growth parallels the organization's growth, and it is your responsibility to invest energy and time on their development.

Paula got it, but she still had questions. How do you know what a worker is capable of beyond what their line manager shares? For example, if she needed a social media plan for a client, she had to find someone who understood how social media marketing works. Beyond that, she wasn't privy to their aspirations, goals, or career trajectory.

That led us to the second step in building a collaborative workplace: identifying the sweet spot—that place at the intersection between a team member's skill set and their growth edge. Once a leader identifies it in an employee, they must make a commitment to look for opportunities to help them develop those skills further. Leadership must be reciprocal: You ask and demand their time, energy, and loyalty to your project needs, and then you owe them something in return: an opportunity to grow.[3]

There are three steps to help both of you get there:

1. **Assess strengths:** Hold a conversation with anyone who joins your project team to understand what they believe they bring to the team, to acknowledge how much you value that

capability, and to clarify the expectations of how that skill will be used to ensure success.

2. **Identify the sweet spot:** Ask everyone who joins your team: What is your personal ambition? Where do you see yourself in a few years? What skills will you need to get there? What would you love to be an expert in, but don't currently have the capability? In parallel, gather data from their direct manager or from other colleagues and stakeholders who work with them to get a sense of their development needs.

3. **Honor aspirations:** Commit to be on the lookout for a place for them to explore or expand, or find ways for them to be more visible on the team or within the company.

In sum, for anyone who joins your team, even temporarily, there are three steps: assessment, alignment, and two-way commitment. Once that baseline has been created, even a directive alpha style is likely to be better received, and if you need to use your position power to respond to client demands or time constraints, the likelihood of it avoiding negative fallout is much greater.

Turning the Group into a Team

By now, Paula had had two major breakthroughs: 1. She recognized the value of sparking multiple power sources; 2. She understood that from her subordinates' vantage point, motivation soars when they connect the dots between their work and their aspirations. Even small chunks of time spent discussing their strengths and how their involvement will further their development would be well spent.

This reframing of her role set us up for my next question. "Just because a bunch of folks come together on one of your projects, do they automatically constitute a team?" I asked.

"Of course," Paula said reflexively. "Once people are assigned to me and we meet to outline a project and agenda for crafting a presentation or proposal, from that moment forward they are on my team, no?"

"Maybe," I said. "But just because you gather folks around a table and give them a timeline and agenda doesn't mean that you have a true team. What's the difference between a team and a group?"

The truth is, there is much debate around the distinction between a functional group and a team. What is well researched, however, are the actions leaders need to take to increase the likelihood that a group will become a team. From my experience and the latest research, there are five critical factors that must be addressed:

1. **Know your why:** If Paula hoped to cultivate an esprit de corps, she needed to connect her agenda with a more emotionally resonant, aspirational message. She needed, as expert organizational consultant Simon Sinek says in *Start with Why*, to share "the why." As a first step, leaders need to step back and take a little time to connect the work with their own deeper values, answering these questions: Why does this project matter? Why do I care? Why should the employees care? Communicating from this place foments the enthusiasm necessary to bond a team, and energizes diverse groups of people—engineers, accountants, salespeople, product designers, you name it—even if only temporarily.

2. **Set goals that work:** In the literature on goal setting, the acronym you see most often is that the most effective goals should be SMART: specific, measurable, achievable, relevant, and time

limited. But what is often neglected is how leader and employee will work together to meet, even exceed, those goals. What resources will the team need? What support mechanisms are in place to ensure success? Far too often, bosses set goals and timetables, then shift quickly into follow-up mode: What has been finished? Where's the update? The result is that the "how" of follow-through (energy, support, feedback) is dropped from the equation, and when a deadline slips or someone fails to make the grade, the leader gets frustrated, the staff member feels demoralized—and precious time has been wasted.

Setting goals is the easy part! Taking the time to identify the sweet spot between the organization's aims and individual growth, to clarify expectations and resources available—this is the conversation that counts. Goals are only a starting point and may need to be discarded or reevaluated all along the way. I have witnessed leaders so attached to their goals that they insist on seeing them through even when the client, or their boss, has moved on to other priorities. We could call this missing the forest for the trees. Goals are only the first step on a learning expedition about what factors make the most difference, and how to have conversations that identify the right goals, address the staff's level of intrinsic motivation, confront misalignment, and commit resources for support.

Smart leadership, not just SMART goals!

3. **Align expectations:** Once a team is starting to gel, it is important to set up operating guidelines. Paula's role at this stage was to establish, in concert with her staff, how conflict would be handled, as well as baseline norms of professionalism, respect, and courtesy.

These sorts of principles are far too often left implicit until there is a blowup or someone behaves inappropriately, which can undermine morale, create chaos, and bring teamwork to a standstill. It is essential for a leader to be explicit about expectations and conduct an open dialogue about how members will treat one another. They also need to walk the talk and model whatever norms they espouse.

One norm that is too often left unsaid until it devolves into a corrosive influence is how people use email and phones. Under stress, leaders are sometimes the first to dispense with pleasantries, or ignore emails and phone calls altogether. Instead, they resort to texts that are directive and curt: "Did *you* do it?" "Didn't get the note. Where is it?" It's easy to forget that even simple text messages, which we all use, come across with emotion, whether that's frustration or impatience, even if unintentionally. They're ubiquitous and easy, but can be amazingly destructive. It is ironic how often these so-called smart tools wind up as the dumb messengers.

The solution to using tech for quick, transactional communications is to be smart about it, and cautious: If emotions are driving your fingers when they hit the keyboard or the dial pad—stop. We all know that texting while driving is a big no-no (and illegal in many places!), and texting while rushed, angry, or anxious is an equally likely setup for an accident. Always remember, as the leader, you set the tone. Be sweet when you tweet.

4. **Implement feedforward:** As we've discussed, millennials typically value feedback. They want to know whether they're doing work that both satisfies their own needs and the needs of

the team. The mistake many companies have made is relegating the feedback process to an annual, formalized human resources procedure. To get the best out of people, research indicates that ongoing feedback is much more valuable and much more motivating—even if it's constructive criticism—when timely and specific, rather than given at the very end of the project, or a year later. My most successful clients set up ongoing feedback conversations, sometimes weekly. One e-commerce client designated every Friday morning as a "Feedback Friday," during which team leaders are expected to evaluate one area of development and growth for a member of their staff. [4]

Paula already knew the value of feedback; she took the time to get input from her clients on a regular basis. She often ended sessions by asking them for one area or item that they wanted her team to focus on or do differently. Unbeknownst to her, she had been utilizing a form of feedforward all along. She indicated her clients loved this approach because it reinforced that, at the end of the day, she was committed to listening to their needs.

Now it was time to extend that same consideration to her staff.

5. **Create a safe space:** The next step is to reflect on whether you are creating a psychologically safe environment. Harvard Business School researcher Amy Edmondson has studied this topic over many years, especially in the health care arena. Her main takeaway: The key to success, even when there is a clear hierarchy, is that explicit permission has been given for anyone to speak up. As I've observed working with surgeons and anesthesiologists in the OR, where highly trained experts come together for short, intense spurts of activity, collaboration is crucial to a positive

result. The attending surgeon and her residents may be the ones in action, but everyone's role is honored, and everyone's voice is heard. In short: Safe operating rooms produce healthy patients.

Psychological safety, according to Edmonson, means that:

- People feel able and encouraged to *speak up*.
- People are encouraged to reach across functional boundaries and trade the power dynamics of leader/ follower in favor of partnerships.
- There is ongoing learning, with regular debriefing, asking, What works? What could we do better?
- There is defined, acceptable risk-taking.

(This last idea of risk-taking, of course, will vary greatly depending upon the team. In a creative environment where the goal is to come up with a new product or innovative approaches, taking risks makes more sense than in the OR.)[5]

Paula thought that discussing psychological safety with her team was unnecessary, because her people would feel empowered to speak up if they saw something going awry.

"Be careful about assuming that junior people, people who are new to your team, or people from other cultures have the where-withal and self-confidence to speak up," I cautioned. "Unless you've made it clear that you value their input, many may feel intimidated. What if someone on your team is an introvert? How will you get the best input if you just assume that everyone can say whatever they want? The extroverts will take over—mostly men, right?"

She laughed. "Just yesterday one of my male team members went off on a rant in front of everyone. He seemed to feel en-titled to just take over."

She was making my point for me: Creating an environment that feels safe and inclusive to everyone—particularly minorities and women—is crucial for today's teams to fulfill their potential and unleash the talents of all their members.

Empowerment Plus: Coaching and Mentoring

It finally dawned on Paula that succeeding at building a high-performing team would be as complex as convincing a client to buy into one of her proposals—and just as rewarding. She was ready to move on to the final, and perhaps most important, element to bolster and fuel her team: shifting her mind-set from delegating and directing to empowering, via coaching and mentoring—which in and of itself can be a difficult distinction to parse.

Both mentoring and coaching means supporting someone to learn and grow, but they use fundamentally different sources of power. In a mentoring conversation, the dynamic is constructed around mentor expertise: transmitting knowledge and wisdom from someone with experience to someone at a lower level. Like all forms of teaching, this relationship inherently involves a "power over" construct.

Coaching, on the other hand, is ideally a partnership in which, even if the coach is the boss and the coachee a subordinate, when in coaching mode, that hierarchy is minimized. The leader shifts her perspective from the knowing elder to supportive colleague. The focus is on supporting the coachee to become more aware of their own capability to problem-solve, determine their personal aspirations, or recognize blind spots. That flattening of the pecking order can be difficult or awkward for a leader, especially if they want to have a feedback or goal-setting meeting. Feedback can certainly be part of the coaching dynamic, but to be effective in that context it must emphasize the positive—that is, look at what works instead of what's broken. As neuroscience has shown, there's nothing more demotivating than a leader kicking things off with negative feedback.

Paula could see where being clear about the coaching conversation, environment, and timing would be crucial if she wanted her team members to come away excited and committed to change. Even if a session is just a few minutes, or you find yourself switching hats in midstream from coach to mentor and back again, it is essential to step back and consider context and how safe your coachee or mentee feels to speak up. As with everything else we've examined, collaboration has a strong somatic component. If you feel stressed or frustrated, your colleague will hear it—and see it—loud and clear.

Ultimately, the words you say and the questions you ask, no matter how well crafted, may be the least important component of effective coaching. I told Paula about a senior executive who held coaching sessions with minimal success, even though he did a lot of prep work, asked open-ended questions, focused on the positive, and attempted to come across as more of a colleague than a boss. He was doing all the right things, except one: He conducted the coaching sessions while leaning back in his high-winged chair, arms behind his head, feet up on his huge desk.

"I get it," Paula said. "No matter what my boss says to me, no matter how inspiring, if he's leaning back with his feet up on the desk, I will know he's just going through the motions. He's not really focused on my personal growth. He's just doing the boss thing."

The details matter.

The Quiet Leader

You may be wondering, "If I'm already a beta leader, can I skip this section?" Yes and no. It's true that it is less common to find a beta leader who struggles with collaboration, but not as rare as you might think, and their challenges can be just as daunting. If you are a naturally good listener, consensus oriented, and inclusive, you may be able to enhance your approach even further. There are at least three types of beta leaders who become their own worst enemies when it comes to collaboration: consensus builders, whose ardent passion for dialogue leads to endless discussions without conclusion; brainstormers, who can never get enough creative ideas (we'll meet someone like that in the next chapter), leaving their team feeling unguided and overwhelmed; and introverts, who hold themselves back, naturally feeling more comfortable letting others speak, thus often relinquishing their role as leader. Simply put, you can have too much of a good thing. Blessed with the collaborative gene, betas sometimes overuse it.

A former high school teacher, now assistant principal at a Manhattan charter school, Kendrick was the kind of principal that we all wish we had in high school. I wound up working with him to refine and optimize his already strong cooperative skills. He wasn't an introvert, but he was an extremely good listener, and he preferred to empower the teachers to come up with their own resolutions to the organizational and discipline issues that came up. But when I met them, I could tell by their body language—eye rolling, crossed arms—that they were frustrated with his lack of guidance. Ironically, his intention to empower ended up making them feel just the opposite whenever he would abdicate his leader role, leaving them to figure things out on their own.

Kendrick was generally viewed by his staff as trustworthy and a positive role model, but he needed to up his game. His challenge was to be clearer about his personal vision, to articulate goals for himself and the team. To go back to that distinction of coach versus mentor, he was already a great coach to his teachers, but there were times when he needed to be a mentor, too, and provide them with a road map for success, not just dialogue.

Whenever I find myself across the table from a highly empathetic, diplomatic, often introverted manager, we wind up focusing on what might initially feel counterintuitive or go against their instincts: They need to take up more space. They've gotten far by listening and leading with persuasion rather than directives, but they hold back in situations where visibility might be important for the success of the team.

I love to refer introverted leaders to Susan Cain's excellent book *Quiet: The Power of Introverts in a World That Can't Stop Talking*, which I mentioned before. I remind them that the only way our culture will expand to welcome a broader array of leadership styles is if they stand out, at least on occasion! Cain is herself an introvert who never set out to do a TED Talk that would be seen by millions, and she has since discussed how challenging it is to speak on behalf of that substantial portion of the population who would prefer to hang back and listen rather than be in the spotlight.

Quick-Hit Workout: Alpha to Beta

1. **Power down:** Reflect on the types of power you are employing. Add a new one to your repertoire by finding a role model who uses it well; ask them how, when, and why they switch things up. Consider what it means to be a leader-follower, and look for opportunities to upend the hierarchy: Empower others to lead *you*.

2. **Power across:** Imagine concentric circles around yourself and evaluate how well you leverage your networks and stakeholders. Consider the potential benefits of collective leadership models. Where can you expand the circle?

3. **Identify sweet spots:** Investigate your own strengths and the strengths of your team. Ask each team member to identify their sweet spot and help them make an explicit plan for future learning and growth.

4. **Distinguish between "mentor" and "coach":** Note the "power over" dynamic of mentoring and the "power with" model of coaching. Know the difference and do both. Ask yourself, "Am I the expert giving advice (mentoring), or am I an equal exploring and identifying options (coach)?"

5. **Build in safety:** Pay attention to the timing, body language, and context in which you collaborate. Ask yourself, "Am I available and listening? Am I encouraging others to speak up? Am I turning mistakes and failures into learning? Am I simply trying to be right or looking to explore options and grow?"

Quick-Hit Workout: Beta to Alpha

1. **Power up:** Optimize team dialogue and feedback sessions: Be directive and focused, have an agenda, get everyone to engage, and don't leave yourself out. Clarify the purpose of each meeting and vocalize your goals and intentions up front.

2. **Buddy up:** Team up with a peer who is more directive and make a commitment to coach each other. Get them to spend more time and energy on dialogue, to get better at listening and non-verbal behaviors, while you commit to discipline, efficiency, and directness.

3. **Stretch out, reach out:** Ask yourself, "What activity could I engage in that would feel like a stretch, and broaden my visibility and impact?" Make a commitment to build your network,

even if only one person at a time. Building a network of collaborators is not about quantity but continuous expansion and depth of connection.

Building a Collaborative Culture

As we've seen, many leaders are tossing out the old-fashioned org chart altogether and replacing it with experimental models that flatten hierarchy, spread power among team members, and leverage the network. There is an emerging awareness, even among corporate scions, that to achieve new levels of growth they need *the best ideas*—and ideas, as we know, are not the exclusive province of the top. Some companies, including the shoe company Zappos, have even taken steps to dismantle the ladder altogether, adopting a holacracy instead, in which employees rotate in and out of project circles, sharing leadership and applying skills where needed.

The postindustrial information age is waning, and the age of creativity is ascendant. The evidence-based drivers of employee motivation we discussed earlier—autonomy, relatedness, competence—means that building a culture of collaboration is paramount. Whether carried out in a holacracy or some other emergent structure, the nature of the workplace is changing. Today's flatter organizations are asking employees to lead and collaborate more—from wherever they sit.

As the chair of surgery at Rutgers University Medical School recently remarked to me, "In the operating room, the surgeon may still sit atop the pyramid—after all, she wields the knife—but when we study outcomes, we can see that teamwork is vital." It has been a revelation for me to observe that particular culture change—surgeons becoming coaches—in action. It hasn't always been easy. As one of the doctors shared with me, "We are trained to be perfectionists in the OR. We follow rigorous methods, or people die. Coaching is much more nuanced—I'm never quite sure I'm doing it right!"

I reminded her, "When I observed an operation, what struck me was the level of listening, attentiveness, and energetic presence brought to bear by everyone in the room. That's all it takes to be a great coach as well. You guys do it, in spades, every day."

The future is bright for organizations, no matter how entrenched in their hierarchies, when they are willing to put in the time and effort to build a culture of collaboration. It's not about trying to be perfect, but a willingness to show up and be present every day.

CHAPTER 10

Be Engaged: From Above and Below the Neck

On the morning of June 4, 1943, Irv Culver, who worked under engineering lead Clarence "Kelly" Johnson at the Lockheed Aircraft Corporation, was likely reading "Li'l Abner" when he answered the phone, "Skonk Works here," referring to the rundown factory in the highly popular comic strip. The call was from Navy headquarters in Washington, and Kelly fired Culver on the spot. Later, Culver was reinstated in his job, the Skonk Works story spread—and the name stuck.

At the time, Johnson's aeronautical engineering team was secretly developing an entirely new jet fighter plane from scratch, the XP-80 Shooting Star, for the U.S. government, and they did it seven days ahead of schedule. It became legendary. In his autobiography, Johnson shared fourteen rules for running a "skunk works operation," the philosophy that underpinned the success of the project. "Skunk works" has since come to describe a small group of creative types tasked with developing new applications or products in an unstructured environment, unhampered by bureaucracy. Today a skunk works doesn't need to be off in some undisclosed location. In fact, it could easily describe the stated philosophy of most start-ups, and the innovation divisions of huge companies such as Amazon, Google, and Facebook.

We are all skunks now.

Today's leaders can create skunk works in any organization. After all, why should only a select few get to work on their islands of creativity? It's time to redefine work itself, so *all* the skunks among us can investigate, dream, and solve the often intimidating problems facing humanity. In this chapter, we'll look at how you can be the kind of leader who creates a skunk works–style team of innovators just about anywhere—in the middle of a *Fortune* 500 firm or at a tiny nonprofit, and everywhere in between. The key to success is unlocking the genius in everyone!

These days, whenever statistics come out on employee engagement, the results are almost always dismal. Despite the media's obsession with fun-loving, entrepreneurial businesses becoming the backbone of twenty-first century America, HR reps are all too familiar with surveys like these: Gallup and CCL (Center for Creative Leadership) have found that only 13 percent of employees worldwide—and only 27 percent in the United States—feel engaged at work. The findings are based on surveys of worker satisfaction, work-life balance, retention, and other data that indicate whether employees are happy. Obviously, the answer is no.

If you consider the level of engagement that creative types put into their work, whether it's software engineers, writers, actors, or musicians, most will tell you that happiness or satisfaction is a rather alien measure of their level of engagement: what they exhibit is passion, and most important *purpose,* a commitment to expressing themselves in the world. When it comes to these surveys, we may be asking outdated questions based on antiquated definitions of work itself. These days, workers will likely have four or five careers in their lifetimes, but most companies have not fostered the kind of flexibility that enables reinvention—and that's a shame. Employers that encourage growth and don't insist on rigid job descriptions can spark creativity in their workers, engendering continuous learning and making it more likely that their employees will stick around. Some of the most forward-thinking companies are experimenting with cross-functional and even cross-generational initiatives that invite odd bedfellows to connect.

One example of this kind of breakthrough thinking took place at the staid two-hundred-year-old insurance company The Hartford. The organization's executives, mostly baby boomers, saw the tidal wave of Facebook, Twitter, and Instagram but were unsure what to do about it. When a small group of early career professionals (millennials and Generation Xers) also noticed that The Hartford was not adapting quickly enough to emerging technologies, they initiated a roundtable to discuss how the insurer could better incorporate social media, mobile Internet, and intranet communications. In response, the CEO launched an unprecedented reverse-mentoring program in which an early career mentor is paired up with an executive mentee to discuss new technologies and how they might be used at the company. Naturally, the mentee—as a senior leader—is also able to teach the mentor about the business and provide career advice and development feedback. Mentors and mentees regularly get together in groups to share their learning as well.

The HR team that oversees this cross-generational collaboration has noted several positive outcomes already, even after only one year. The first is the heightened engagement and development of young professionals, who are at a higher risk for turnover. Secondly, The Hartford has updated its social media usage and policies and increased access to technology tools. Finally, since this is an ongoing program, senior leaders have access to fresh ideas, and employees gain knowledge early in their careers about how a major corporation is run. It is truly a win-win dynamic for a firm that was in need of reinvention and a younger generation in need of a reason to stick around.

A Dose of Alpha for a Beta Max

As soon as I entered the conference room, the dissonance hit me. I'd been hired by Jonathan, the executive director and founder of a digital media consultancy, to coach the head of IT/innovation, head of operations, and head of research. When I first met them all together, it was clear that chaos reigned. I should not have been surprised: The unstructured, fluid, sometimes contentious behavior of the team was very much by design. Jonathan had one goal: innovation. His vision was to accelerate social change via digital media products. His approach to this lofty goal was simple: Hire brilliant and specialized young professionals—software engineers, data science analysts, culture and media research mavens, social psychologists, and neuroscientists—and let them loose to generate ideas, applications, and products that would change the world.

So why enlist the help of a coach? For one, the team was perpetually behind on deadlines. As Jonathan admitted, they lacked the one thing needed to enhance their creativity: discipline. The question he grappled with was this: How could he maintain a culture of risk-taking while also focusing on results? He had already tried hiring a director of operations, Kathleen, who was very much his opposite. But in the collegial culture he had fostered, any hint of "power over" leadership was met with resistance.

It turned out Jonathan had one significant blind spot: He, and he alone, had set that tone. His freewheeling style, rambling brainstorming sessions, tendency to disappear for days on end, and general disregard for planning or follow-through led the team to believe that deadlines didn't matter. When I entered the scene, brainstorming had turned to venting, as Kathleen tried desperately to get everyone to be more accountable. Jonathan was about to fire Kathleen; Kathleen was about to quit; the research team and data scientists were frustrated by what they saw as "too much oversight from Kathleen, too little direction from Jonathan"—and Jonathan was at his wits' end.

Our first sit-down meeting occurred on the heels of one of the team's free-for-all planning sessions, "Monday Morning Madness," as they called it, where I had a ringside seat to their boisterous interactions.

"There's no question that you have an engaged group," I said.

Jonathan sighed. "Engagement is not my problem. Everyone is passionate and hardworking. We just have so many ideas—and so many projects in the pipeline—that the one idea that we really need gets neglected."

"What idea is that?"

"Ah." Jonathan sighed again. "The idea that deadlines matter."

I showed him the results of a recent study of high-performing engineering teams at Google.[1] The top five values they reported were:

1. **Psychological safety:** It is okay to speak up, share mistakes, and focus on learning rather than blame.

2. **Dependability:** Leaders are consistent in their values, behavior, and commitments.

3. **Structure and clarity:** Leaders set reasonable expectations and time frames for execution, and there are clear lines of accountability.

4. **Meaning:** The work connects to what employees care about most.

5. **Impact:** The work matters.

Jonathan got good marks for numbers 1, 4, and 5, but we had work to do on 2 and 3—no surprises there. He told me that he had always been what he liked to call a "surfer" through life, recognizing from an early age that he could procrastinate and still come out successful, so it wasn't obvious how he could inject discipline into his day-to-day. I asked him to think back to a time when he could remember demonstrating discipline or structure.

"In high school," he recalled, "I ran for class president because everyone told me that I would win. I was a good athlete; I was friends with just about everyone. But the night before I had to give my campaign speech, I got stressed; I hadn't done any of the actual work. In the wee hours of the morning, I came up with a very specific list about the importance of teacher-student relations, budgets for expanded arts programs, stuff like that. I guess I do have the ability to be disciplined; I just resist using it. I want to get the best ideas out of my staff, and I don't want them to feel stifled."

"The last thing you want to do is relinquish the environment of creativity that has helped you build innovative organizations again and again," I agreed. "But as you can see from the research, and as you can hear from your team, it's important to balance it with other capabilities."

Over the next few months, Jonathan expanded his style, adding a touch of alpha to his well-honed beta ways. Always inclusive and democratic, he suggested that we work with the whole team to determine what must change. He was sensitive to how having a coach would be perceived—"Here comes the guy who is going to turn Jonathan into a tyrant"—so I was on board with involving key colleagues. They set goals for Jonathan and the overall workplace. We ultimately agreed on the four I's—elements of leadership and organization that everyone concluded would optimize productivity while not undermining creativity:

1. **Inject discipline:** Keep *brainstorming sessions* only for brainstorming. The team agreed to short, open meetings with a focus on one or two questions at a time.

2. **Inject clarity:** Hold separate *productivity sessions*—structured meetings focused on project plans, timelines, and commitments. Separating their meetings was a real shift; previously, the creative energy of a brainstorming session could quickly dissipate when the topic turned to accountabilities.

3. **Inject structure:** Jonathan agreed to *clarify expectations* in one-on-one conversations with each key team member by writing down reciprocal commitments that outlined how their personal goals, strengths, and growth opportunities would dovetail with the agenda of the organization.

4. **Inject collective wisdom:** *Have everyone lead.* This fourth and final injection of new energy required Jonathan to explicitly define accountabilities, responsibilities, and ownership of specific deliverables for all team members. In other words: Everyone needed more alpha spirit, so they wouldn't just rely on Kathleen for it.

This last point is crucial, especially when it comes to coaching. Jonathan, like all of us, was surrounded with potential coaches. Only by agreeing on how each team member might wear a wider array of hats was it possible for Jonathan both to step out of the leader role and follow along, and for Kathleen or another alpha talent to coach him, and vice versa. By the time our work was over, the commitment to coaching one another in ways that would elevate the discipline and productivity of their colleagues had become a new norm within this maverick culture.

At the end of the day, Jonathan was still Jonathan, and the open, unfettered space of creativity that he nurtured was still alive and well. What we accomplished together was to inject small cultural shifts that made all the difference, turning a skunk works into a productivity machine.

Big Pharma Takes Its Own Medicine

We move now to the other end of the spectrum, the field of biopharmaceuticals, where I had an opportunity to work with a leader charged with engendering innovation and creativity in his company. When I first sat down with alpha Amar, he told me how his team of scientists was coming up with exciting ways to solve diseases stubbornly resistant to man-made drugs. One of the fastest growing areas of research in the industry, "biopharmaceuticals" refers to the use of natural molecules and compounds, sort of the organics of the pharma world, to design and manufacture medicine for some of our most debilitating ailments—cancer, diabetes, Alzheimer's. Scientists are also uncovering and extracting the powerhouse healing capabilities of Mother Nature herself.

Amar was running a skunk works inside a huge multinational,

which, if it had been successful, would have reinforced my theory that it's possible to lead a team that's both highly creative *and* highly productive pretty much anywhere. The problem, as I would shortly discover, was that even though his team was both super-creative and got results, their productivity came at a price. Unbeknownst to Amar until I collected feedback, most of his subordinates were not just disengaged; they were miserable. Many of them were looking for other opportunities. Some told me they were on the way out as soon as they could find another position, while others had become resigned to feeling overworked and under-recognized. Still others shared that as much as they loved the science and appreciated their brilliant peers, they resented the subculture of mistrust and competition, and felt oppressed by a pervasive sense of threat and insecurity: If they didn't come up with the next great idea they would lose out on rewards and recognition.

Amar was vaguely aware of a lack of engagement—in fact, it's why he had reached out for help. Fortunately, he was receptive to exploring how he could reinvent his leadership approach, learn to flex, and discover ways to inspire his people to reignite their enthusiasm for innovation. I suggested that before we jump into exploring what was going on with the team, he share with me how he nurtured his own creative side. His energetic presence would be essential: The leader sets the tone. He told me that his best ideas emerged when he was relaxed, reflective, and able to detach from the nitty-gritty.

"It's a struggle," he said, "because even though my instinct is to give my team a great deal of freedom and flexibility, we are still a results-oriented organization. There is a lot of pressure on me to deliver."

"But if that pressure is resulting in burnout and low morale, then your skunk works is not exactly operating on full tilt," I reminded him.

He agreed. "It saddens me to think that we're not fully leveraging the talents of my amazing scientists, chemists, tech wizzes, and biologists."

"Aha! You just used the key word: 'leverage.' In the most successful creative endeavors I've seen, leaders seek to create an environment that leverages everyone's full potential. It starts with realizing that you can't force creativity—as you already know about yourself."

I walked him through what I call the "six levers of engagement," which a leader needs to pull to get the most out of their talent pool. Start by visualizing the office environment as a series of concentric circles emanating outward from an individual team member. Why? Because, if you think about it, where do all great ideas start?

When I asked Amar this question, he had an immediate answer. "All great ideas are generated from an insight or breakthrough from one or a handful of the brains I've gathered on my team."

"No matter where you are when the idea hits—in the shower, walking, daydreaming, brainstorming—what one thing do all of them have in common?"

"I guess they come when I'm feeling positive, right?"

"Bingo! Great ideas emerge in those moments when we feel inspired, enthused, vital, and alive."

The word here was "feel." Surrounded by scientists and engineers, it was easy for Amar to fall for the myth that creativity starts in the brain—but it is simply not true. Consider the word "motivation," which comes from the Latin *motere,* to move. When we are moved by music, art, nature, or beautiful ideas, we're talking about feelings. That's why the six levers of engagement start with the one that matters most: the heart.

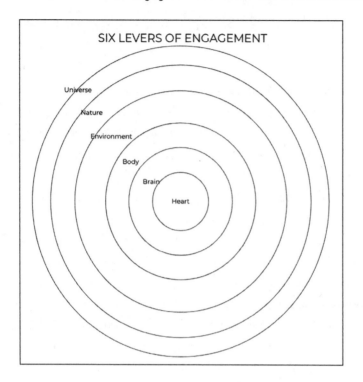

SIX LEVERS OF ENGAGEMENT

Universe

Nature

Environment

Body

Brain

Heart

1. Leverage the Heart

We have already discussed myriad ways a leader can connect with and touch the hearts of others: Adapt your style to the context, be a great listener, practice curiosity, know your why, communicate with feeling, focus on the positive, express feelings openly, be vulnerable and humble about your fears, build trust and safety, coach and mentor, and create a culture of collaboration. This all made sense to Amar on a rational level, but I could tell there was a huge obstacle to his taking up these recommendations—and, as you might imagine, it "gets to the heart" of what prevents many leaders from stepping up their games as well. For Amar, at this challenging moment, leadership itself felt like work. The pressure to be a good boss had drained him of the very thing he was supposed to instill in others: inspiration. He was also burned-out.

Motivating a team of skunks in the middle of the factory is tough. But it points to the fundamental theme of this book: Coach yourself first. Amar needed to step back, give himself a break, literally and figuratively, and reconnect with his why. Why did he become a scientist in the first place? What still excited him? What got him out of bed in the morning? To model the kind of vitality and enthusiasm that he needed to instill in his team, he had to start by reconnecting to, and re-enlivening, his own heart.

I asked Amar to think about areas where he had neglected the nutrients that he needed to sustain and revive his body and mind. What he most needed was rest, and space and time for reflection. A short vacation was in order—a rare feat in his fast-paced, demanding environment, but necessary. He even agreed to leave his laptop at home (of course, he could still check his email on his smartphone). When he got back, he brought renewed energy and commitment to what he most loved about his work. He gathered his team together and inspired them with stories from his early days as a researcher uncovering the healing properties of organic compounds that ultimately saved thousands of lives. It was not a job but a calling—and he just needed to refresh his own passion to transmit that same message to his team.

2. Leverage the Brain

The brain is our most mysterious organ. We don't know the core mechanism of consciousness, or how humans translate language into meaning or vice versa. On the other hand, there has been a great deal of neuroscience and neurobiology research that gives us a window into what occurs in the brain when creativity occurs. Dr. Carlos

Davidovich, an executive coach, physician, and expert in neuromanagement techniques, has determined the best ways to achieve creative insights from a neurological point of view. He advocates activities that balance the brain's use of energy and accelerates connectivity, including: 1. interspersing short creative spurts with rest—chunks of downtime and naps; 2. taking walks or exercising, since creativity is spurred by body movement; 3. not *trying* to be creative, but rather scheduling time to let the mind wander, reflect, drift; 4. staying positive, not punitive.[2]

3. Leverage the Body-Mind

The third lever requires looking beyond the brain to what I call the body-mind, that special elixir of physical and emotional energies that combine to foster creativity. As discussed in chapter 8, the science of intuition—gut insight—is proving that breakthrough thinking is as much a physical and emotional process as a cerebral one. It's crucial for the body to be in a state of balanced energy—not bored or complacent, but also not revved up with anxiety; the environment must feel safe.

Safety, belonging, and trust are more than just concepts; they are energies with somatic, emotional, and cognitive elements—and all must be present if we are to feel empowered to try out new ideas, especially if they feel risky or outside the box. The truth is, getting "outside the box" is well-nigh impossible, as we all live in multiple boxes: body, workplace, family, state, nation. What we can do is make those boxes more expansive and more inclusive to set the groundwork for ingenuity and inspiration.

So Amar first attended to issues related to physical and emotional balance, starting with diet, nutrition, sleep, and exercise. Then he started to connect the dots between innovation and a healthy, open environment. Studies are beginning to demonstrate with evidence that creativity can happen not just inside of us but within the *energetic network that flows between us,* which I find really thrilling.[3] For example, studies have shown a "network effect" with coaching; when one individual in a group gets coached and then follows through on new practices, greater self-awareness, and other energetic shifts, he winds up having a nonlinear yet direct impact on the attitudes and behaviors of the folks around him. Those aftereffects of coaching can impact the energy, culture, and creativity of an entire company.

4. Leverage the Environment

The fourth lever that leaders need to pull extends the concentric circle beyond the brain and body into the environment. As we discussed in chapter 8, research has shown that the spaces in which we work have a direct connection to vision and resourcefulness. It is important to pay attention to both time and space. We all know that some people do their best work early in the morning, some late at night. But our workplaces tend to be stuck in an outdated narrative that pushes people into time-space boxes, where "work" is supposed to occur in a glass-boxed cubicle under fluorescent lights, between nine A.M. and five P.M. Does this really optimize creativity for most of us? It's important to pay attention to the balance between public and private, aesthetics, and the freedom and autonomy of each worker to choose the environment that will foster their vitality. Some will want solitude and quiet to do their best work. Some will want to brainstorm and bounce ideas off others. Some find the energy of dialogue sparks their greatest insights.

Here are four activities leaders can do to make the most out of the work environment: 1. Expand the definition of work time to accommodate people's biological clocks; 2. Attend to the aesthetics—soft colors, natural light, fresh air, soothing textures—of the work space; 3. Incorporate a mix of public and private spaces; 4. Create inviting getaway spaces that celebrate and cultivate relatedness (for example, coffee-bar-style hangouts with comfortable seating).[4]

5. Leverage the Natural World

The fifth lever takes us beyond the work space into the world. The world around us is extraordinary complex, beautiful, and mysterious. We are not just in the world, but of it—and we forget that at our peril.

Numerous studies have demonstrated that spending time in nature has a restorative effect, reducing stress and lowering cortisol levels in subjects who spent as little as thirty minutes a day walking in a forest. Most of us know that time outside has a powerful impact on our heads, hearts, and souls. For a leader trying to unleash creativity in her people, finding ways to practice mindful engagement with nature—whether it's through walking meditation, hiking, or wandering in a wildlife sanctuary—might just spark a connection, or bring forth an insight, that changes the world.

How a corporate team takes up this challenge may not be immediately obvious, but it could be as simple as walking out the door. Amar was initially unable to generate any ideas of how to get his people out of their cubes and into the great outdoors, as wonderful as it sounded. But when he asked his team for suggestions, they chuckled. Many of them were already taking regular walks in the forested foothills surrounding their corporate campus in eastern Pennsylvania.[5]

6. Leverage the Universe

The sixth level of the concentric circle of engagement I like to call "leveraging the universe." Whether it is breathing in the vast ocean of stars on a clear night—and remembering that you are just as likely to be *looking down* at them, as up—or peering through a microscope at a human cell only to discover that it is a mirror reflection of that same starry night, the core of this lever is activating your sense of wonder. We need to continuously revisit our assumption that only a portion of the population is creative. We are all artists at birth. It's so important for leaders to stay connected to the vast unknown, to tap into their spirit of exploration.

Over the months that we worked together, I noticed a head-to-toe change in Amar's physical demeanor. He seemed to be getting younger and younger right before my eyes! As he nurtured his brain, his body, and his soul, his creative juices once again began to flow. He could still fall back on being authoritative when needed, but as he allowed the little boy in himself to come out and play, work became fun again.

At the end of the day, being able to flex from alpha to beta and back again is all about energy. The framework above is designed to help you refocus your energetic approach to your team. Think about what levers you have the power to pull—and be playful! Experiment. The good news is that none of us have to lead alone. Just as Jonathan benefited from empowering and then following his team's alphas, Amar also had role models in his midst. He just had to seek out the betas and invite them for a walk in the woods.

Quick-Hit Workout: Alpha to Beta

1. **Start with heart:** Connect with your inner purpose—whatever motivates you every day—and practice speaking from that place.

Get your team to do the same, and share what gives your work meaning, in both formal and informal settings.

2. **Build on the brain:** Cultivate practices based on neuroscience that energize the brain's natural creativity: Take regular breaks, work in focused chunks, allow the mind to wander, and reinforce small steps forward with celebration.

3. **Foster creative spaces:** Pay attention to the environment and the timing in which creativity flourishes; experiment with solo and group brainstorms; leverage the power of one—and the network of many.

4. **Foster trust:** Attend to the nuances of interpersonal relationships: avoid punitive judgments, be a role model for vulnerability, consider mistakes as opportunities for learning.

5. **Invoke wonder:** Be playful and open to possibilities; honor the mavericks (especially the quiet ones); bring touchstones (toys, kaleidoscopes, Legos, musical instruments) into your work space to remind you to see the world through the eyes of your inner child.

Quick-Hit Workout: Beta to Alpha

1. **Clarify expectations:** Discuss explicit goals and support mechanisms, such as coaching, mentoring, or training, needed for each team member. Ensure that goals are mutually agreed upon and achievable with a stretch; incorporate plans for ongoing learning and growth. A good rule of thumb is to create a context whereby everyone can "work themselves out of a job" over time, so there is continuous reinvention of the role and the individual.

2. **Inject discipline:** Create consistent practices that everyone signs on to: meeting times and agendas, operating principles,

regular updates (what form and how often), and a process for setting deadlines. Consider this written operating agreement—like the U.S. Constitution—to be binding on all, but amendable as needed.

3. **Imbed structure:** Determine a configuration that supports role clarity, asks for leadership and accountability from everyone, and remains flexible. Define boundaries in ways that support individual autonomy while building on interpersonal connections and trust.

4. **Leverage the collective:** Unleash the genius of the group in playful, unstructured activities (games, events, nature experiences) that encourage new combinations and break down functional silos. Include time for debriefs, reflections, and shared learning.

5. **Celebrate learning (not just wins):** Find ways to have peers recognize one another publicly for learning and growth; make celebrations a regular part of the work experience—not so often they become routine and not so rare that they are too little, too late.

Lightning Strikes Twice

As we bring our journey together to a close, I want to acknowledge the amazing clients who have joined me in the pages of this book. Having taken up the gauntlet of leadership in today's crazy, upside-down world, they are my heroes, role models, and teachers. In these pages, you have met leaders of all stripes—men, women, people of color, LGBT professionals, millennials, boomers, and Xers—all with one thing in common: a willingness to be a student, to be coached and to coach themselves, to shine a light on their blind spots, and expand their repertoire in service of the lofty goal of optimizing their potential and that of everyone they lead.

Looking back on the very first case study that led to my creation of the FIERCE framework, you may be asking yourself whether Mark was a freak of nature. Perhaps you came away thinking that it takes an Ivy League education and a surgeon's acumen to nurture the multidimensional capabilities—flexibility, intentionality, emotional agility, authenticity, collaboration, and engagement—that research shows are key to effective leadership in today's flatter, wired world. Let's visit with one final leader, from the other side of the tracks—and dispel that myth forever.

When I first met Allen, the CEO and owner of a hundred-year-old family business that designs and manufactures high-end Plexiglas furniture, I thought I had stepped through a time warp. Under the screeching of high-powered saws and drilling machines, a floor thick with wood chips and dust, workers cutting, gluing, polishing, and packing—a whirlwind of sweaty humanity—it all seemed to be running like clockwork, even without anyone visibly in charge. But there he was: shoulder to shoulder with his floor supervisor, going over plans, debating project timelines, shouting above the din, and walking the floor with nods of approval and high fives. Allen was in the mix, enthusiastic, engaged: a somatic leader par excellence.

Later, in a marketing meeting, Allen posed open-ended questions and patiently took notes as his team grappled with issues big and small. He was receptive, inquisitive, a consensus builder. He could switch modes with ease and authenticity, from "power over" his employees to "power with" as the context required. From plant floor to boardroom, he knew how to change the tone of his presence, his communications, and his demeanor to get the best productivity and creativity from his team. Despite the chaotic urgency of the plant floor, he seemed calm and attentive as coach and facilitator during staff meetings, with a physical presence that came across as respectful and attentive. Allen knew that stressing his team out with pressure about sales or budget demands would shut off the juices that produced the creations in his showroom. Furniture can be bland and practical, or it can be designed with flair, and it was the latter that kept his firm alive and thriving.

Observing Allen, I knew that what I had witnessed in the operating room with Mark was not a fluke. If a hundred-year-old New York factory can simultaneously be a high-productivity machine and a skunk works for innovation, then a theory of leadership that transcends the alpha-beta split, integrates task and relational dynamics, and leverages the collective talents of all is not a pipe dream. With a realistic and humble recognition of his strengths and flaws, Allen had honed his team into a flexible, purposeful, engaged collective of passionately committed workers.

Lathe operators from El Salvador worked thirty feet away from Swedish design students, Jewish customer service reps, an Indian accountant, and an LGBT millennial sales manager. Over lunch in a nearby Greek diner, Allen brought them together regularly to recognize their efforts, to stimulate dialogue and cross-functional learning, and to celebrate accomplishments—meeting sales targets, unveiling new designs, going months with no factory floor accidents. In sum, thanks in part to Allen's FIERCE leadership, the melting pot is alive and well in America.

My fundamental belief is that everyone who picks up this book has the potential to be FIERCE enough to lead like Mark in the operating room or Allen on the factory floor. Today's innovators need to transcend silos, break through boundaries, and coach themselves to be multifaceted—a fully realized leader, engaged partner, willing follower. As you look to continuously push against the edge of your own limitations, your goal must be to break down any wall that blocks you from knowing yourself. Don't worry about climbing ladders that no longer exist. Instead, seek to defy the laws of gravity by elevating yourself and all of those around you with your passion, creativity, and enthusiasm. As simple as it sounds, you can be an inspiring leader, live out your deepest dreams, and change the world—from wherever you sit. And you can start right now.

Epilogue:
The Call for Belonging

As I write these words, spring is finally appearing (a bit late) in the Catskill Mountains outside New York City, and despite what I shared in the pages of this book, it is not lost on me that we live in incredibly polarized times. At the very moment that I put forward my thesis that the next evolution in leadership asks us to move beyond the "heroic" meme, we've seen a resurgence of autocratic, male-dominated political administrations, not just in the United States, but in some of the countries where the next great waves of talent will emerge—China, Russia, Syria, Turkey, Israel, Egypt, and the Philippines.

But I also see organizations across the globe flattening, broadening, and reimagining their structures, elevating women and people of color, and experimenting with networked, distributed, and shared leadership models. And a bit more good news: The number of female, minority, and nonbinary candidates that are running for political offices—at local, state, and federal levels—has surged to new highs.

The glass ceiling of the U.S. presidency may not have been broken in 2016, but many others are likely to be shattered very soon.

In fact, I can't help but wish there were one more letter in the word "fierce": another "I." (Sadly, my bad spelling plus force of will can't turn "IFIERCE" into a particularly memorable acronym.) As I scan the horizon of leadership for signs of things to come, there's one quality that is rapidly on the rise: *inclusion*. It makes sense. One of the core themes of this book is that the outworn tale—that heroic leaders always show up as white knights—is dissembling, losing its grip on organizations around the world. Simultaneously, we are experiencing a *rainbow ascent*: Leaders arrive daily on the scene in every conceivable combination of color, race, gender, sexuality, and culture.

But as important as this topic is to me, I don't by any means consider myself an expert in this domain. For that, I look to such role models as my friend and colleague Jennifer Brown, who speaks, teaches, and writes with eloquence on the subject. Her book, *Inclusion: Diversity, the New Workplace and the Will to Change*, is an important addition to the research. I am moved by Jennifer's vision: "I want us to work within organizations and across society as a whole to dismantle the false binaries and unconscious bias that separate us so that we might celebrate together all the differences that enrich us—while still being aware of the importance of safety in community. Above all, I want each of us to feel welcomed, valued, respected, and heard at work—and in life." The urgency for change is clear, and the future is now.

Carl Jung wrote about human development as a lifelong process he called "individuation," in which each of us continuously constructs and deconstructs the self as we grow into adulthood and beyond. Survival requires a strong ego, as mental models—belief systems, collective values, social norms—provide us a crucial experience of belonging. Jung also points out that those very same ego constructs must be broken apart in the service of growth. Rigidity, brittleness, and breakdown are all signs of a psyche in transformation. Just as the skin of a snake dries up, peels away, and leaves the snake raw and exposed, we are making way for a new skin—our new, inclusive human story.

We live in an age of convergence—of liminality—during which much of what has passed for normal has ruptured, and the only constant is change. Liminality represents what psychologists refer to as a "threshold": a time of transformation when the old way has not been fully vanquished and the new identity of the individual or community not yet fully formed. As leaders in this space, we are called to embrace paradox, to break apart mental models and beliefs that no longer serve us. Those who can surf the wave of change without being pulled under will lead the way. My call to arms is for us all to learn to *flex*—and to strive to be inclusive.

Together, let's build a world where anyone can lead—as everyone must.

ACKNOWLEDGMENTS

The odd fact about a book is that it typically appears emblazoned with only one name, as if the author holed up in cave (with a laptop) and walked out six months later, hardcover in hand. In reality, the book you hold in your hands was only made possible because of a multitude of teachers, collaborators, researchers, clients, friends, and family who blessed my writing journey with their wisdom and support. It is with great humility and gratitude that I can now reflect on the gifts so many people have given me—of their time, insights, feedback, and love.

The first seeds of what would grow into the FIERCE model germinated in conversation with my dear friend and former business partner, Pascal Scemama, a wise soul whose amazing life journey took him from a top engineering school in France to a manufacturing plant in Michigan to a trading floor on Wall Street—and, thankfully (for me), to an early foray into leadership consulting. Along the way, Pascal and I developed a deep passion for supporting leaders—becoming "leadership coaches" long before coaching had even been named as a profession. Pascal, ever the adventurer and visionary, became a Harvard-trained anesthesiologist at the age of forty. Soon thereafter, he introduced me to Mass General Hospital in Boston, where I worked with some of the smartest, most agile leaders I had ever encountered. Pascal, it is an honor to have you now, and forever, as partner, confidant, and friend.

I want to thank Jeanine Wiener-Kronish, Harvard professor and the Chair of Anesthesia, Critical Care and Pain Medicine at MGH, for believing that I could make a difference with her team of high-powered doctors. It was here that I came to believe that if a safe, flexible, emotionally intelligent team of leaders could be nurtured in the operating room, it could be developed anywhere.

It was also while working at Mass General that I met Carol Kauffman and Margarete Moore, founders of the Institute of Coaching, the Harvard Medical School–affiliated research institute that would catapult my belief in the power of coaching to a whole new level—providing me an amazing team of colleagues with whom to collaborate and expand my thinking. To Carol, Margaret, Susan David, Irina Todorova, Chip Carter, Kelly Standel, Laurel Doggett, Sue Brennick, Stephanie Girard, and the entire team at the IOC, I am deeply grateful. Without their thought leadership and camaraderie, this book would never have been possible. Also, a special note of gratitude to Ruth Ann Harnisch, whose generous support made the Institute of Coaching possible—and whose funding, coaching, and empowering the next generation of women leaders inspires me every day.

If you are perusing these acknowledgements after reading *Flex*, then you already know that I have been blessed with an amazing variety of coaching clients from just about every demographic, age, industry, function, and size. I could not even begin to thank them all. There is a profound reciprocity in being a coach: I always learn as much from my clients—probably more—as I offer them. Many of my favorites ended up in the pages of this book. It is their leadership journeys—trials, tribulations, wake-up calls, and ultimate successes—that made the whole endeavor worthwhile.

I have also been blessed with an abundance of professional partners—many of whom have brought me with them into far-flung leadership programs around the globe. With deep appreciation, I want to acknowledge Tracy Duberman at TLD Group, Annie Abrams and Thuy Sindell at Skyline Group, Juan Jose Callejas, Terrill Thompson, Cuc Vu, Nicole Cozier, Leslie Jaffe, Anna Flores, Gabriele Ganswindt, Haesun Moon, Eric Kauffman, Eileen Fracchia, Jan Rybeck, Andreas Bernhardt, and Ben Croft. It has been and continues to be a joy to play with you!

The act of writing a book is a solo event—but crafting a beautifully designed product that wends its way into the hands of readers, as they say, takes a village. My publishing "village" has been comprised of a team of brilliant professionals. My patient and persevering agents, Sonali Chanchani and Frank Weiman at Folio, stuck by me through multiple iterations of the proposal and many gyrations with publishers, always believing that the ideas in this book would find a home and get out into the world. They were right, of course, and I wound up blessed with a supremely talented team of editors. Stephanie Bowen, Nina Shield, and Harriet Bell helped sculpt *Flex* into its current form, bringing their insight, patience, and most importantly, sharp but gentle carving knife to my rather verbose writing. I am deeply appreciative of their support.

Working full-time as an executive coach, writing a book, and supporting the IOC all at the same time left me little time to investigate and conduct what this book sorely needed—good evidence-based research. For that I was once again blessed, as Liz Dantzker, Columbia grad student and research assistant par excellence, came to my rescue. And as a coach myself, I'm always aware of the potential benefits of having a good one, so I got lucky when I discovered Jennifer Wilhoit way out in the wilds of Washington State—a talented writer, nature lover, and writing coach extraordinaire. Thank you, Jennifer, for your early morning promptings to get up from my desk and out on to the land, even if only Central Park—to touch the earth, breathe in fresh air, and revive my creative spirit.

When I reflect on the profound impact so many teachers, researchers, and thought leaders have had on my thinking, it strikes me as impossible to thank them all. But some stand out and deserve recognition, for their words have permeated my soul and expanded my thinking, often when my own solutions to a leadership conundrum didn't hold up. Many of them found their way into *Flex*. On their shoulders, I stand: Carl Jung, Margaret Wheatley, Pema Chodron, Marshall Goldsmith, Ryan Niemiec, Dan Goleman, Simon Sinek, Susan Cain, Jennifer Brown, Richard Strozzi-Heckler, Richard Boyatsiz, Susan David, Margaret Moore, David Peterson, Tom Lutes, Allen Schoer, Gifford Booth, Reuven Bar-On, Tatiana Bachirova, David Rock, Amy Edmondson, Barbara Fredrickson, Barbara Kellerman, Martin Seligman, and Carol Dweck. You are my heroes.

I may have looked to the teachers above for guidance as I wrote, but when it came to testing ideas, grappling with tone, choosing the right words, or just lifting me out of a writing funk, it was my dear friends and a few special family members who tolerated my endless riffs on the crumbling patriarchy and the emergent leadership landscape. To Barbara Phillips, Steve Mendelsohn, Judy Fox, Polly Howells, Xavier Roux, Maura Conlon-McIvor, David Frechter,

Hudson Talbott, Andrea Lowenthal, and Kurt Andernach, thank you for your love and support. Your friendship means everything to me.

There is one person (and two beautiful cats) who kept my life grounded, sane, and energized through multiple drafts and then the despair of hearing that I had written enough for *two* books on the first go-round and had to chop, chop, chop (which, thanks to Nina and Harriet, turned out to be totally right)—my life partner, Jason. For those late-night glasses of white wine that magically appeared on my desk, to warm hugs at difficult moments, and his steadfast belief in me and the message of this book—I am eternally grateful.

Finally, last but hardly least, a nod to my graduate students at NYU, whose diversity, intelligence, and creativity give me hope for humanity, even as populist, authoritarian, and ethically dubious leaders rise to the top of some of the most advanced democracies—ours included. Democratic institutions around the world are clearly in a perilous state. Yet the young leaders, from all over the world, that attended my classes, are strong, vibrant and *FIERCE*, and as they take over the reins of power from what will hopefully be the last generation of autocrats, I remain cautiously optimistic. This book is for them

NOTES

CHAPTER 2

1. **Neuroscience studies of feedback:** Neurologist and educator Judy Willis conducted brain research that indicates student learning is inhibited when the classroom environment is stressful and teaching methods are focused on negative feedback loops. She writes, "Neuroimaging and measurement of brain chemicals (neurotransmitters) show us what happens in the brain during stressful emotional states.... When stress activates the brain's affective filters, information flow to the higher cognitive networks is limited." Bottom line: The brain shuts down in the face of negative feedback—and responds to positivity by engaging all the networks that foster motivation, creativity, and a willingness to try new things. See J. A. Willis, "Connecting Brain Research with the Art of Teaching," *School Administrator Journal of AASA*, School Superintendents Association, September 2017; http://my.aasa.org/AASA/Resources/SAMag/2017/Sep17/Willis.aspx.

2. **Positivity ratio studies:** Research by Barbara Fredrickson found in multiple studies that college students with a positivity ratio above 3.0

237

(three or more positive emotions for each negative) were significantly more likely to have high mental and social health. Although there continues to be debate in academic circles about the specific quantitative measures and application of "positive emotional expressions," Frederickson's basic theme—that positive emotions have a direct impact on the quality of relationships, health, and performance—continues to be cited and confirmed in additional settings (for example, in nursing home patients). Fredrickson's "broaden-and-build" hypothesis suggests that the broadened attention afforded by positive emotion prompts engagement in an expanded repertoire of behaviors that ultimately prove adaptive by enabling people to recognize and take advantage of new opportunities. See B. L. Fredrickson, "The Role of Positive Emotions in Positive Psychology: The Broaden-and-Build Theory of Positive Emotions," *American Psychologist* 56:3 (2001): 218–26; http://dx.doi.org/10.1037/0003-066X.56.3.218.

3. **The neuroscience of isolation:** Studies by A. M. Stranahan at Princeton University found that social isolation can exacerbate the negative consequences of stress and increase the risk of developing psychopathology in the brain. By studying the impact of individual versus group "housing" on the brains of rats when both are provided opportunities for exercise (normally a positive influence on brain health), they discovered that when isolated from one another, even the positive action of running had a negative impact on brain function of rats. Rats, like humans, are social animals, and brain experiments of this type suggest that social isolation has a deleterious impact on brain functioning. See A. M. Stranahan et al., "Social Isolation Delays the Positive Effects of Running on Adult Neurogenesis," *Journal of Nature Neuroscience* 9:4 (April 2006): 526–33; http://dx.doi.org/10.1038/nn1668.

4. **The neuroscience of accomplishment:** Dr. Joe Z. Tsien, co-director of the Brain and Behavior Discovery Institute at Georgia Health

Sciences University, discovered that key receptors for dopamine function in the brain operate as "gateways" that are essential to enable habit formation. Dopamine is a key neurotransmitter that is released when people feel a sense of goal accomplishment—it is known also as the "reward molecule" that fuels positive motivation based on pleasurable feelings evoked when individuals exercise, complete basic tasks, meet deadlines, and form positive habits. See J. Z. Tsien et al., "NMDA Receptors in Dopaminergic Neurons Are Crucial for Habit Learning," *Neuron* 72:1 (2011): 1055–6; http://dx.doi.org/10.1016/j .neuron.2011.10.019.

5.   See Carol S. Dweck, PhD, *Mindset: The New Psychology of Success* (New York: Penguin Random House, 2016).

CHAPTER 3

1.   **The importance of listening:** In a study of leadership practices at a Norwegian hospital, Erik Oddvar Eriksen and his co-researchers from the University of Oslo found that successful leadership depended strongly upon managers assuming what they termed a "communicative mode" of interaction. Their study refuted past research where the emphasis was on an "instrumental" view of leadership focused on efficiency and goal achievement. Researchers found that leaders who created an environment of mutual understanding and problem-solving through active dialogue—and listening—were considered more effective than managers who focused on efficiency and goal achievement through sanctions and rules. See E. O. Eriksen, "Leadership in a Communicative Perspective," *Acta Sociologica* 44:1 (2001): 21–35; https://doi .org/10.1177/000169930104400103.

2.   For a good summary of listening perspectives from a top executive coach, see Carol Kauffman and William H. Hodgetts, "Model Agility: Coaching Effectiveness and Four Perspectives on a Case Study," *Consulting Psychology Journal: Practice and Research* 68:2 (June 2016): 157–76.

3. For more information on Tatiana Bachkirova's work on the multiplicity of self, see Tatiana Bachkirova and Simon Borrington, "The Limits and Possibilities of a Person-Centered Approach in Coaching Through the Lens of Adult Development Theories," *Philosophy of Coaching: An International Journal* 3:1 (May 2018): 6–22; https://doi.org/10.22316/poc/03.1.02; and Tatiana Bachkirova, *Developmental Coaching: Working with the Self* (London: Open University Press, 2011).

4. **Mindful leaders make better leaders:** Maree Roche at the University of Waikato in New Zealand and her colleagues studied the role of mindfulness on the well-being of leaders. Utilizing four samples of 205 CEOs/presidents, 183 middle managers, 202 junior managers, and 107 entrepreneurs, they tested the direct effect that their level of mindfulness (heightened awareness) had on their mental well-being. In all four samples, it was found that mindfulness enables them to view situations "for what they really are" without rumination or worry of past or future negative events. They concluded, "Rather than being mindless and frantic, present moment awareness and attention allowed the leader to focus on the issue at hand, not on the problems that may arise, or have previously arisen, allowing them to facilitate reflective choices . . . that benefit their mental health and well-being." See Maree Roche et al., "The Role of Mindfulness and Psychological Capital on the Well-Being of Leaders," *Journal of Occupational Health Psychology* 19:4 (October 2014): 476–89; https://doi.org/10.1037/a0037183.

5. **Neuroscience of curiosity:** According to researcher M. J. Gruber and colleagues at the UC Davis Center for Neuroscience, curiosity helps us learn about a topic, and being in a curious state also helps the brain memorize unrelated information. This research provides insight into how piquing our curiosity changes our brains. Participants in the study first rated their curiosity about the answers to a series of trivia questions.

Later, they had their brains scanned while they learned the answers to those questions. People were better at learning the trivia information when they were highly curious about it. The investigators found that when curiosity is stimulated, there is increased activity in the brain circuit related to reward. The team also discovered that when learning was motivated by curiosity, there was increased activity in the hippocampus, a brain region that is important for forming new memories. See M. J. Gruber et al., "States of Curiosity Modulate Hippocampus-Dependent Learning via the Dopaminergic Circuit," *Neuron* 84:2 (October 2014): 486–96; https://doi.org/10.1016/j.neuron.2014.08.060.

CHAPTER 4

1. **Better storytellers get more $$:** Researchers at Concordia University and the University of Alberta conducted extensive analysis of start-up companies in biotech, Internet, and the semiconductor industries, specifically examining how the narrative approach taken by the founders impacted the likelihood and amount of funding they received from investors. They found that entrepreneurs who were skilled storytellers—articulating a strong sense of identity, vision, and values—were funded at higher levels than firms that focused exclusively on business models and financial projections. See M. L. Martens et al., "Do the Stories They Tell Get Them the Money They Need? The Role of Entrepreneurial Narratives in Resource Acquisition," *Academy of Management Journal* 50:5 (October 2007): 1107–32.

CHAPTER 5

1. See Thuy Sindell and Milo Sindell, "7 Ways Women Leaders Can Excel Being Their Authentic Selves," *Skyline Group* (blog), September 2017, https://skylineg.com/resources/blog/7-ways-women-leaders-can-excel-being-their-authentic-selves/.

2. For further information on the work of psychologist Dr. Reuven Bar-On, his most recent publications, and the development of the emotional intelligence assessment, the EQ-i 2.0, see http://www.reuvenbaron.org. If you are interested in taking the EQ-i 2.0 assessment yourself, you can learn how to connect with a certified practitioner through MHS Assessments at http://www.MHS.com or reach out to the author: jeff.hull@instituteofcoaching.org.

3. **Left/right brain a myth:** Scientists at the University of Utah have debunked the myth with an analysis of more than one thousand brains. They found no evidence that people preferentially use their left or right brain. Dr. Jeffrey Anderson, director of the fMRI Neurosurgical Mapping Service at the University of Utah, and his team examined brain scans of participants ages seven to twenty-nine while they were resting, studying, problem-solving, and exercising. They looked at activity in seven thousand brain regions, and examined neural connections within and between these regions. Although they saw pockets of heavy neural traffic in certain key regions, on average, both sides of the brain were essentially equal in their neural networks and connectivity. See J. A. Nielsen et al., "An Evaluation of the Left-Brain vs. Right-Brain Hypothesis with Resting State Functional Connectivity Magnetic Resonance Imaging," *PLoS ONE* 8:8 (2013): e71275; https://doi.org/10.1371/journal.pone.0071275.

4. **SDT and effective leadership:** Anthony J. Amorose and colleagues at the School of Kinesiology and Recreation, Illinois State University, used self-determination theory to study whether perceived competence, autonomy, and relatedness impacted the motivation and subsequent performance of student athletes. They surveyed 581 male and female high school and college athletes about the degree to which they perceived their coaches to be autonomy supportive, confidence building, and interpersonally related—and determined that these

factors had a significant impact on the motivation of students to improve. See Anthony J. Amorose and Dawn Anderson-Butcher, "Autonomy-Supportive Coaching and Self-Determined Motivation in High School and College Athletes: A Test of Self-Determination Theory," *Psychology of Sport and Exercise* 8 (2007): 654–70; https://doi.org/10.1016/j.psychsport.2006.11.003.

5. **Neuroscience of SCARF:** Neuroscience researchers at UCLA have identified neural systems responsible for experiences of pain and pleasure, such as being accepted or rejected, treated fairly or unfairly, and esteemed or devalued by others. The pain network associated with sensory aspects of physical pain (for example, its location in the body), is activated in the same way during periods of emotional distress. It turns out, likewise, that having a good reputation, being treated fairly, and being cooperative all activate similar brain networks employed in the experience of physical pleasure. The brain's reward circuitry receives the neurotransmitter dopamine: the same chemical and networks employed in the experience of desirable foods and drinks. See M. Lieberman and N. Eisenberger, "Pains and Pleasures of Social Life," *Science* 323 (February 13, 2009); http://www.sciencemag.org.

6. **Antagonistic neural networks:** According to Case Western University psychologist Richard Boyatzis, when a test subject's brain activity is mapped through fMRI imaging while focused on task-oriented activity, the TPN (task-positive network) is engaged, whereas the DMN (default-mode network) associated with relational/emotional activities is suppressed, and vice versa. This dichotomy reflects a "tension between empathetic and analytic reasoning," and it appears that the brain is challenged to simultaneously process the social and emotional aspects of leadership while solving analytical problems. This neural network polarization of roles has problematic implications for leaders. As Boyatzis states, "Developing a leader's analytical and

relational abilities may be important to offset the effects of this 'antagonistic' brain dynamic. . . . The ability to switch between networks and corresponding leadership roles may prove to be key for leadership effectiveness." See R. E. Boyatzis, K. Rochford, and A. I. Jack, "Antagonistic Neural Networks Underlying Differentiated Leadership Roles," *Frontiers in Human Neuroscience* 8:114 (2014); http://doi.org/10.3389/fnhum.2014.00114.

CHAPTER 7

1. **Vulnerability as a strength:** Researchers at the University of Nevada School of Environmental and Public Affairs interviewed and analyzed data from educational leadership doctoral students who were participants in a simulated work environment training that asked them to risk a level of personal discomfort and engage in personal reflection. They found that when training programs created an environment that fostered a safe space for self-disclosure, participants became much more engaged, learning focused, and consequently committed to leading others with greater sensitivity in the real-world setting of their organizations. Edith Rusch et al., "Transforming Leadership Identity in a Virtual Environment: Learning About the Leading Self," *Journal of Transformative Education* 11:1 (2013): 45–69.

2. For more in-depth analysis of the neurological functioning behind facial recognition, resonance, trust, and nonverbal connections between humans, see research by Paula Niedenthal, professor of psychology at the University of Wisconsin–Madison. For example: Paula Niedenthal et al., "Functionally Distinct Smiles Elicit Different Physiological Responses in an Evaluative Context," *Scientific Reports* 8 (2018); http://doi.org/10.1038/s41598-018-21536-1.

3. **Values alignment key to trust in leadership:** At the University of Queensland, researchers investigated the relationship between leadership practices and trust in scientific and technology staff on research

and development teams. Three factors proved to be most important in building trust in leadership: transparent communication about decision-making, communicating a collective vision, and sharing common values with the leader. According to researcher Nicole Gillespie, "Sharing common values helps team members predict how the leader will act in the future, and gives them the assurance that the leader is unlikely to act contrary to the shared values. Shared values, shared goals, and consultative decision-making reduce uncertainty, as it requires open, honest communication and sharing of what is important to each individual." See Nicole Gillespie et al., "Leadership and Trust: Their Effect on Knowledge Sharing and Team Performance," *Management Learning* 41:4 (2010): 473–91; https://doi.org/10.1177/1350507610362036.

4. **The leadership value of humility:** Researchers at Ohio State University, Portland State University, and Renmin University of China identified leader humility, characterized by being open to admitting one's limitations, shortcomings, and mistakes, and showing appreciation and giving credit to followers, as a critical leader characteristic relevant for team creativity. They explored the relationship between leader humility and team creativity, treating team psychological safety and information sharing as variables. Data was gathered from 72 work teams and 354 team members and supervisors/managers from 11 information and technology firms in China. Results indicated a positive relationship between leader humility and the value, impact, and approach to information sharing. In addition, researchers found that openness and transparency in information sharing on the part of leaders helped build psychological safety, which led to significant elevation of team creativity. See J. Hu et al., "Leader Humility and Team Creativity: The Role of Team Information Sharing, Psychological Safety, and Power Distance," *Journal of Applied Psychology* 103:3 (2018): 313–23; http://dx.doi.org/10.1037/apl0000277.

1. **Science of somatic intelligence:** Jon Hindmarsh at King's College and Alison Pilnick at the University of Nottingham, UK, conducted a video-based study of anesthesia work teams, analyzing organizational members' physical bodies in action. The research highlights the importance of intercorporeal (somatic) knowing in the real-time coordination of teamwork. Observing senior physicians at work, the researchers noted that teams coordinate complex clinical and physical movements, in concert, using minimal verbal interaction. Signals such as body placement, gestures, enactment, and facial expressions—nodding, smiling, eye contact—demonstrate that even in highly complex team interactions, bodily conduct and nonverbal communications underpin the "talk" of organizational members and are critical to their success. See Jon Hindmarsh et al., "Knowing Bodies at Work: Embodiment and Ephemeral Teamwork in Anesthesia," *Organization Studies* 28 (2007): 1395–416; http://dx.doi.org/10.1177/0170840607068258.

2. Taisen Deshimaru, *The Zen Way to the Martial Arts* (New York: Penguin, 1982).

3. **Body as language:** Associate professor Alison O'Malley and colleagues at Butler University set up an experiment where they had observers watch a video of a leader engaging in a series of approach, avoidance, or neutral behavioral expressions during a speech while the observers' physical reactions were recorded by a web camera. Results demonstrated that observers were more likely to mimic avoidance behaviors (for example, crossing the arms, shaking the head from side to side) than approach behaviors (extending the arms, nodding the head), based on the physical gestures they observed; observers were highly attuned to nonverbal activity, mimicking the behavior without conscious awareness. Additionally, observers who

engaged in avoidance mimicry tended to have a negative impression of the leader compared to those who observed a more approach/open style of nonverbal behavior. See A. L. O'Malley et al., "Incorporating Embodied Cognition into Sensemaking Theory: A Theoretical Integration of Embodied Processes in a Leadership Context," *Current Topics in Management* 14 (2009): 151–82.

4. Carrie Arnold, PhD, PCC, "The Silenced Female Leader: Coaching Women to Find Purposeful Voice," Willow Group, April 2017; http://www.willow-group.com. Research sponsored by the Institute of Coaching, McLean Hospital, an affiliate of Harvard Medical School.

5. **Science of intuition:** A team of researchers at the University of New South Wales scientifically demonstrated the existence of intuition—what we think of as "gut" decision-making. In the experiment, college students were shown clouds of moving dots, which looked and sounded like "snow" you might see on an old TV. Participants had to decide which general direction the cloud was moving—left or right. Subjects were asked to make decisions while photographs with positive images, like adorable puppies, as well as negative images, such as a snake about to strike, passed before their eyes (without them being aware of them). Pearson and colleagues found that participants' decisions were directly impacted by the images. The researchers also measured participants' skin conductance—an indicator of physiological arousal—as they made decisions, noting a significant physiological reaction to the emotional content of the pictures—even though when surveyed, they all agreed there had been no photographs. Their startling conclusion: Unconscious "data" impacts the body and the brain and absolutely informs—and can even improve—our decision-making. See Galang Lufityanto et al., "Measuring Intuition: Nonconscious Emotional Information Boosts Decision Accuracy and Confidence," *Psychological Science* 27:5 (April 2016): 622–34.

6.   Richard Strozzi-Heckler, *The Art of Somatic Coaching: Embodying Skillful Action, Wisdom, and Compassion* (Berkeley, Calif.: North Atlantic, 2014).

7.   **The environment matters:** James C. McElroy at Iowa State University studied the impact of a major office change/renovation and move of employees within a large Midwestern financial services organization. An online survey was administered to 271 (35.4 percent male and 64.6 percent female) employees, roughly half of whom had participated in an office redesign and relocation project. The company undertook office renovations with explicit goals: reduce costs by housing more employees in less space, promote a more collaborative culture, and increase positive work-related attitudes. All new furniture was purchased, the décor was updated, brighter colors were selected, and partition height was decreased to allow for increased natural light. Common meeting/gathering areas were created and existing noise was decreased. Results indicated that employees exposed to the new office arrangement viewed the organization's culture as less formal, more innovative, and more collaborative, and felt they had a greater sense of autonomy. See J. McElroy, "Employee Reactions to Office Redesign: A Naturally Occurring Quasi-Field Experiment in a Multi-Generational Setting," *Human Relations* 63:5 (2010): 609–36.

8.   Jennifer Wilhoit, PhD, *Writing on the Landscape: Essays and Practices to Write, Roam, Renew* (Bloomington, Ind.: LifeRich Publishing, 2017).

CHAPTER 9

1.   Rockwood Leadership Institute; https://rockwoodleadership.org /art-of-leadership/.

2.   **Collaborative leadership works:** A group of researchers set out to answer the question "Does collaborative leader behavior result in better decision-making?" The experiment was conducted over a seven-month period with MBA graduate student teams who met in a

sequence of one-hour blocks to make academic guidelines decisions with team leaders (trained actors) described as key school officials— deans, professors, and administrative execs. The researchers set up two sequential sets of meetings, with the "leaders" leading students through a similar decision-making process using two radically different styles of leadership behavior. One group of leaders behaved in classic alpha mode with their teams: interrupting them with directives and consistently making power demands and "I"-based statements. The other leaders were trained to be collaborative in their approach: ask open-ended questions, encourage their teams to speak up, and use open, welcoming physical gestures (tracked with sensors) that demonstrated empathy, transparency, and co-powering energy. The results were resoundingly clear: The more participative the team dynamic, the more likely the group decision was reached with consensus and was the "right" one. The upshot: Collaboration works. See Kim T. McFee et al., "Sociometric Badges: Using Sensor Technology to Capture New Forms of Collaboration," *Journal of Organizational Behavior* 33:3 (2012): 412–27.

3. **Jumping the S-curve:** Paul Nunes and Tim Breene, leaders of Accenture's high-performance business research program, studied thousands of companies from scores of industries around the world, demonstrating that many leaders manage their companies only focused on the so-called S-curve of revenue growth—in which a business starts out slowly, grows rapidly until it approaches market saturation, and then levels off. Top-performing organizations, by contrast, actively manage hidden S-curves continuously and early, so as to overcome disruptions and prepare for next-generation innovation. A key finding in their research was the S-curve of talent development—the importance of building a hothouse of talent to do what labor markets alone cannot. What this looks like in practice: Companies such as Schlumberger invest heavily to obtain a steady flow of

talent, then provide continuous learning through coaching, training, job rotations, and job expansions so that employees consistently "jump" their personal S-curve. See P. Nunes and T. Breene, *Jumping the S-Curve: How to Beat the Growth Cycle, Get on Top, and Stay There* (Boston: Harvard Business Review Press, 2011).

4. **The neuroscience of positive feedback:** Research conducted by Richard Boyatzis and associates at Case Western Reserve University identified subtle changes in the brain patterns of students who undergo fMRIs while exposed to a video of themselves responding to questions and feedback that generates a positive emotional versus negative response. According to Boyatzis, "The positive emotional attractor" (a neurocortical network activation) triggers constructive cognitive and physiological responses that enhance an individual's motivation, effort, optimism, flexibility, creative thinking, resilience, and other adaptive behaviors. The "negative emotional attractor" (a different cortical network in the brain) triggers a separate process that elevates social stressors and may compromise an individual's effectiveness. While both emotional attractors play an important role in intentional change, it is key to focus on the positive to enhance intrinsic motivation for change. See Richard Boyatzis et al., "The Role of the Positive Emotional Attractor in Vision and Shared Vision: Toward Effective Leadership, Relationships, and Engagement," *Frontiers in Psychology* 6:670 (2015); http://dx.doi.org/10.3389/fpsyg.2015.00670.

5. **The benefits of psychological safety:** Amy Edmondson, Novartis Professor of Leadership at Harvard Business School, studied the performance and team dynamic of sixteen operating room "interdisciplinary action teams" in cardiac surgery comprising surgeons, anesthesiologists, nurses, technicians, and support staff. She concluded that team learning and performance was substantially enhanced— greater efficiencies, greater success at implementing new technologies, fewer errors—when the following attributes were developed and

implemented: leaders received coaching to mitigate the negative impacts of hierarchy, team members were empowered to "speak up," and communication sessions were conducted that explicitly sought to minimize differentials in power and status among team members. See A. Edmonson, "Psychological Safety and Learning Behavior in Work Teams," *Administrative Science Quarterly* 44:2 (1999): 350–83.

CHAPTER 10

1. See *New York Times* reporting on the employee surveys and work done inside Google to reinforce its values: Charles Duhigg, "What Google Learned from Its Quest to Build the Perfect Team," *New York Times*, February 25, 2016.

2. **Maximizing creativity:** Benjamin Baird and colleagues in the Department of Psychological and Brain Sciences at the University of California–Santa Barbara studied the benefits of rest and mind-wandering periods—breaks in concentration—and found that students performed substantially better at creative problem-solving when given short rest breaks and time for what they termed "incubation"—unfocused, mind-wandering periods of a few minutes. Data suggest that allowing the mind to wander facilitates greater creative problem-solving. See B. Baird et al., "Inspired by Distraction: Mind Wandering Facilitates Creative Incubation," *Psychological Science* 23:10 (2012): 1117–22.

3. **The coaching ripple effect:** Researchers Sean O'Connor and Michael Cavanagh at the University of Sydney used social network analysis (SNA) to study the potential nonlinear and expanded impact of coaching on the well-being of others within what they described as the "relational network" of coachees. In the study, twenty leaders received eight individual coaching sessions with self-reported and 360-degree feedback (pre and post) results that indicated significant increases in goal attainment and psychological well-being. The SNA discovered that members of the coachee's network—for example,

those identified as being closely connected to those who received coaching—also had a significant increase in positive well-being. See Sean O'Connor and Michael Cavanagh, "The Coaching Ripple Effect: The Effects of Developmental Coaching on Wellbeing Across Organisational Networks," *Psychology of Well-Being* 3 (2013); http://dx.doi.org/10.1186/2211-1522-3-2.

4.   There is more and more research being conducted on how to set up model office space configurations that optimize the needs of employees for both privacy and communal interaction. For an example of a model and case study, see Adel Mohammad A. Binyaseen, "Office Layouts and Employee Participation," *Facilities* 28 (2010): 348–57. http://dx.doi.org/10.1108/02632771011042455.

5.   **The creative inspiration of nature:** Psychologist David Strayer and colleagues from the University of Utah and the University of Kansas looked at the impact of nature on creativity. They found that spending quality time in nature—disconnected from technology—significantly improved scores on validated tests of creativity. The study involved 56 people—30 men and 26 women, who participated in wilderness hiking trips. No electronic devices were allowed on the trips. Of the 56 study subjects, 24 took a ten-item creativity test the morning before they began their backpacking trip, and 32 took the test on the morning of the trip's fourth day. The results: "Four days of immersion in nature, and the corresponding disconnection from multimedia and technology, increases performance on creativity, problem-solving tasks by a full 50 percent," according to Strayer, a co-author of the study. See Ruth Atchley, David Strayer, and Paul Atchley, "Creativity in the Wild: Improving Creative Reasoning through Immersion in Natural Settings," *PloS One* 7 (2012): e51474. http://dx.doi.org/10.1371/journal.pone.0051474.

accomplishments, 49–50
adaptability, 9, 105, 179–80
advising, 26
aesthetics, 220–21
agendas, 60, 65, 75, 77
agility, of leaders, 14–15
aikido, 177–81
alignment
  of expectations, 196–97
  in team building, 194
  with values, 162
alpha leaders
  cerebral, 130–31
  communication and, 89–93
  emotional styles of, 130–34
  in hierarchies, 4–5
  as results-oriented, 5–6
  somatic, 132–34
  in surgical teams, 2–4
  vulnerability and, 148–50
Americans with Disabilities Act, 164
amygdala, 86, 138–40

analytical ability, 24, 89, 102
Arnold, Carrie, 175
Art of Somatic Coaching, The
  (Strozzi-Heckler), 177–78
Asiana Airlines flight 214, 1–2
aspirational communications, 86
aspirations, 24, 194
assertiveness, 104, 109–10, 127
assessments
  in team building, 194
  See also EQ-i 2.0; self-assessment
attentiveness, 185
audience, 32, 95
authenticity
  as emotional power, 15
  human connection and, 148–50
  recognizing, 151–52
  See also realness
authoritative, 23
automatic writing, 145–46
autonomy, 119
availability, 122

Index

Mondrian, Piet, 80
moods, journal of, 108
motivation
    behind goal, 18
    connection and, 120
    drivers of, 205
    intrinsic, 50, 124
multiplicity of self, 62
multitasking, 23, 59, 65

narrative-driven, 24
nature, 183–84, 221
nervous habits, 170–72
network
    building, 204–5
    "network effect," 220
    neural, 102
    power, 190
NeuroLeadership Institute, 113–14,
    120–21
neurological resonance process, 58
neuroscience
    of external inputs, 120
    of feedback, 47
    of motivation, 81
neutral space, 29
Niedenthal, Paula, 151
nonverbal interactions, 30

observation, of others, 151–52
obstructive power, 189–90
octopus style, 127–28, 130–34
open-ended questions, 29,
    74–75, 158
openness, 25, 168
operating rooms, 2–4
organizational models
    flatter, 205, 228
    hierarchical, 4–5
    holacracy, 205
    matrixed, 181, 186, 192–93
    new, 5, 205, 228
    power of influence in, 179

organizations
    becoming adaptable, 9
    internal dynamics of, 181
origin story, 87
Outliers (Gladwell), 4
overachievers, 186
over-tasking, 65–66

partnering, 191
passion, 8, 36, 54–56, 208
patriarchy, 175
Payre, Denis, 82–85
peer-to-peer influences,
    190–91, 204
performance poetry, 85
PERMA model, 47–50
persona, listening, 75
personal power, 189
perspective, listening, 75
pet peeves, 141–42
physical attributes, 168–69
pilot error, 1–2, 4
playtime, 76
polarities, 125
positional power, 189–90
positive
    emotion, 48
    outlook, 107
    psychology, 47–50
post-traumatic stress syndrome, 175
posture, 110, 174
power
    in coaching and mentoring, 200
    influence, 179
    optimizing, 187, 188–92
    over others, 178, 204, 210
    with others, 178, 204
    types of, 189–90
power dynamic, 127
PowerPoint, 90
prefrontal cortex, 85
presence, listening,
    74–75